Spiritual Awakening to a New World

By

Raymond Moyer

authorHOUSE™

1663 LIBERTY DRIVE, SUITE 200
BLOOMINGTON, INDIANA 47403
(800) 839-8640
WWW.AUTHORHOUSE.COM

First published by AuthorHouse 10/23/04

ISBN: 1-4208-0585-1 (e)
ISBN: 1-4208-0586-X (sc)
ISBN: 1-4208-0587-8 (dj)

Printed in the United States of America
Bloomington, Indiana

This book is printed on acid-free paper.

DEDICATION

This book is dedicated to my beloved wife, Marian Moyer, for without her encouragement and help it could never have been written.

Table of Contents

-1-

"Our Father, which art in Heaven . . ."

Let us imagine for a moment that it is early evening and we are gazing rather nonchalantly up into the star-filled sky. As our mind muses upon the mysteries of the millions of twinkling stars and the grandeur far above us, we might suddenly realize that God is also gazing out His window of Heaven into the vastness of space toward us. He would see only a tiny, blue, twinkling speck covered with wispy clouds in an arm of a far-off galaxy, one of billions of galaxies in the universe in which we are immersed.

We can well imagine that it is still a time of deep sorrow in His kingdom as He gazes down upon us, a time comparable to the fall of Lucifer, His Star of the Morning, so very long ago as the story is told. For mankind, too, has strayed afar and has become lost, and God is still standing in sorrow, patiently waiting the return of His prodigal sons - and daughters - and wondering what had gone wrong in His beautiful Plan..

1

We perhaps would visualize Him standing there in His flowing white robe with outstretched arms as if to embrace once more these lost ones so far away. We could perhaps even imagine hearing His voice as He would cry out into the vastness of space, "Oh, My children! I have been waiting so long for you to know and love Me! I gave you so very much; a free will, a reasoning mind, and a bountiful world. My spirit has always been within you to guide you, but you have not listened to it. You have turned to your own ways, to your own leaders, and have forgotten Me."

"All I have asked was that you would subdue the earth upon which I placed you, a beautiful dwelling-place for all my creations. Instead, you created a world for your own pleasures. I gave you herbs and fruits from out of Mother Earth for food, and you have eaten My fish, My fowl, and My animals. I have sent you Avatars to guide you but you have killed them without listening to their guiding words. You have followed, instead, the self-appointed leaders who have enslaved you with their rituals and idle promises, while they built their great palaces and glass cathedrals into which you would bring to them your tithes and offerings."

"They have portrayed Me as an accuser and a vengeful Father. Yet, you have always been My loving children. I have always been your Light and the very Life within you. But all I see is selfish vanity consuming you more and more. You still don't know me."

"Take head, My dear children. I give you now another new age, an age of new hope. Use it wisely. Listen for my voice crying out within you. Seek me, and we will walk together again in My beautiful Garden."

* * * * * * * * *

This, we find, is a portrait of how the majority visualize our Heavenly Father, a SPIRIT BEING dressed in white, with flowing white hair as pictures portray Him. Usually, He is seated upon a throne in His kingdom somewhere in the far reaches of space and surrounded by singing Angels as He looks down upon us.

But is this a true picture of the Deity that we worship? Each of us no doubt has our own portrait in our minds, to bring forth at our designated time and place of worship. But, with so many differing religions and beliefs, each with their many denominations and branches, it is nearly impossible to know which to choose. We can only choose that which fit more closely our own feelings and emotions – and try not to judge another's choice, for each of us has our own inalienable right to worship the God we choose.

This might well be the time for us to ask where and when this worshipping of a deity really began. Did it begin with the story of Adam who seemingly "Knew" God? This was only a mere 6000 years ago according to bible chronology while the history of life forms upon our earth dates back millions of years. Creation itself, the very beginning of time as portrayed in the opening verses of Genesis has been pushed back even farther, to some 13 - 15 *BILLION* years ago, though the pattern of sequence as written is amazingly the same. But our sun had to be formed and our earth cast from it, before the invertebrates, before the fishes, the birds, the animals, and lastly man could be brought forth.

So, we can readily visualize in our mind's eye that time has been lengthened to a far greater period than the 6000 years of bible chronology as taught in our religious world. Myths and legends have filled the history of the many races that have spread throughout the earth, in an effort to explain to the masses the laws of life. Very surprisingly, the theme of these universal stories are remarkably similar from race to race; only the names of the deities are different. But each has its own interpretation of the universal powers attributed to their anthropomorphic God, a *spirit Being* high in the heavens. The Christian religion calls it "God". The Jewish religion calls it "Jehovah" The Islamic race calls it "Allah". But these are only names of identity, and the ceremonies and rituals are in reality only states of initiation and understanding.

It is our duty, then, to strive to understand the meaning hidden in the myths of our own religion and possibly the myths in other religions so that we can bring an end to the continual warfare between beliefs.

We find in our daily lives that it is our own individual desires and our own personal thoughts that truly govern our actions. In reality, however, it should be our intuition and our knowledge of right and wrong that should guide us, that "something" that is tucked away in this material body as our true guide. Jesus called it, "The Father within me, He doeth the work."

Life itself has been a great mystery to us, but finally it is being revealed. In an instant of time a newly born baby is changed from a limp, lifeless form into a crying, kicking, living infant by a tender slap on the bottom. Something unseen enters with its first gasping breath. From whence did it come? The DNA explains the complexity of the body. But nothing explains the soul. All we realize is that the brain slowly awakens to consciousness and in a very short time this infant begins to move, to utter sounds, and to reach out for food as its intuition begins guiding it.

Soon its conscious mind begins to take charge with cries and "cooing" as it begins to see the world around it. It begins to be conscious of being an individual. Within a year it has learned to crawl and take a few shaky steps and its world grows larger. From a tiny seed another human has come forth, and within it is an instinct that dates back into antiquity that still guides it until its mind can develop to take charge.

There must be more, then, of a meaning to life that we have never been told existed, far more than just "Eat, drink, and be merry". This brings us face to face with many questions that have never been answered. *"Why* are we here? *Why* are we born under so many different environments and consequences? *Why* are some born to rich families, while others are born into destitute conditions? *Why* are some born into a family of a certain religion and belief that usually becomes our choice, though thousands of beliefs and denominations exist? *What* is the purpose of millions of lives being born each year, to face the hardships of life for a salvation in a nebulous Heaven, or a future of eternal torment? *How* did these beliefs really begin?"

If we believe that there is really no rhyme nor reason to life, then we are in that state of mind that invariably leads to the lifestyle we see all about us. "Eat, drink, and be merry, for tomorrow we SHALL die. The only sure things in life are death and taxes." This, seemingly, is the concept under which we live.

Yet, we can find the inspiration in the Holy Books that should lead us to a better life, to love one another, and most important of all, to "Seek, and ye shall find." We find also the stark reality within the pages of the bible, in book of Proverbs that tell us, "Where there is no vision, the people perish. . ".

We find that there has always been a nucleus of people down through time that has had a vision of a better world, a better way of life, and has felt the urge to search for the answers to these many questions that have never been answered by the clergy. This searching has brought a new understanding of life so that we no longer must try to believe the great untruth that all men are created equal that has been thrust upon us for so long. We are beginning to realize that changes in thought, in beliefs, and in daily life are coming over our world as we reach another milestone in our history. A new century has been opened to us, and with it has come even a new millennium. The closing century becomes only another memorable page in the annals of our past, while the new century opens Pandora's box to a future of both hope and apprehension, according to the aspirations that each of us choose to follow.

With this new millennium a new Renaissance of knowledge and thought is coming forth. A world of scientific technology is shining on the horizon, filled with many glorious revelations and promises far beyond our wildest dreams. The old, tight stranglehold that the Industrial Revolution has had upon our economy for the last century has been loosened. It, too, brought a drastic change in our society as the manufacturing era brought its new ways of life. People began moving from the slow pace of farm life to the crowded, faster pace of big city life and a 9-to-5 job.

Now we are again coming into a new age of change, and it is coming upon us at a much faster pace than we ever imagined that changes could be. Our minds must learn to accept the fact that our old ways and our old beliefs must also fall away for our new hopes and dreams to become a reality. There is the premonition that it will bring us far greater changes than just another new year beginning, for we are also entering a new, mysterious era. Twenty centuries, 2000 years, will have gone by since the birth of Jesus of Nazareth, the child who was declared to be "The savior of the world", and since then the world has gone through many changes at a compounding rate.

Many vision this to be the dawning of the new era that was predicted to come and that man has longed for down through the ages. We cannot begin to visualize at this moment, however, what this new century can bring us. Knowledge has literally exploded during the twentieth century just concluding as we opened the secret world of the atom and saw the very heart of form, the Plus and Minus of energy. We also looked deep into the far reaches of space and saw a universe of unbelievable dimensions We rocketed to the moon. Our probes into space have circled the other planets in our solar system, and even now we are planning for man to land on Mars and again on the moon.

A new concept of thought has also arisen, both in the material world in which we live, and in the religious world in which we worship. Many new questions have arisen regarding our beginning. Many answers have also come forth to clarify our old thoughts and beliefs that reach far back into ancient eras. Acceptance, of course, of these new thoughts has not always been widespread and this is understandable, for we each have our freedom of belief and way of life, as it should be. Each of us must work out our own "salvation" (with fear and trembling) as St. Paul admonished us in his writings in Philippians 2:12.

The consuming desire within us for more of everything, however, has grown equally as fast as the Homo Sapiens mind continues to create new vistas for the toys and possessions that this vast materialistic world now offers. These desires are leading us onward and upward in materialistic knowledge as we gaze into time unknowable, but also allowing us to slip away from the spiritual realm of higher aspirations for a better world for all. We are becoming more and more Individualistic instead of charitable and loving one another as our religions should lead us.

In the Christian world many feel the time is drawing very near that will bring the return of Jesus, the Rapture of the Saints, and the end of the world as prophecies have been interpreted.. There is talk of the Anti-Christ also arising very soon. Others vision that it could well be the beginning of a new, miraculous age, perhaps even the Age of Brotherly Love, when the lion will lie down with the lamb in perfect peace and our weapons of war will be turned into plow shares and pruning hooks, as spoken of in the bible prophecies. It could be an age, perhaps, when robots will be our servants far more than they are today, and we can finally rest and enjoy the fruits of our past labors, each under their own fig tree.

It will not happen in an instant, of course. Much depends upon the mind of man and the direction he chooses to follow, for we have become God-like, knowing both Good and Evil and have even become the Creator of our own world in so many different ways.

So we can only speculate what this new era will bring. Each of us has our own vision of our own little kingdom. But already there is that deep, uneasy feeling of a drastic changing world never before dreamed of as our knowledge keeps expanding and our imagination grows, opening the doors to the new and exciting opportunities ahead.

But we must be "born again" as Jesus taught, into a new concept of thought and deed. Our salvation is far more than repentance, baptism, and accepting that Jesus died for our sins as we have been taught. There must be a new personality arising from out of the old, led by the "New Commandment" given us by Jesus, "Ye must be born again", and "that ye love one another."

8

The world is filled with religious beliefs and dogma that has utterly failed to bring a new and better way of life for the masses who long for it. We are finding that we are certainly not created equal. The time for a new renaissance has come, a new awakening to the possibilities of a new and better world for all.

The twentieth century opened the heavens to us and brought us a new understanding of the beginning, both of time and of life. We were finally shown beyond a shadow of a doubt that millions of galaxies stretch out over an ever-expanding universe we never imagined existed. We see only a small portion of our own Milky Way galaxy with our unaided eyes though it reaches 100,000 LIGHT YEARS across, but our huge telescopes and listening devices have finally proven Copernicus and Galileo correct in saying: the earth and the planets circle the sun!

The computer world and the wireless communication systems have already brought many drastic changes to our way of life, and it is only yet in its infancy. What more can come? We cannot begin to vision the vast number of opportunities that will be available if we follow the proper path, or the terrible cost that might lie ahead if we choose wrongly. This new millennium has brought us face to face with the facts of life that we can no longer evade.

The political world is failing. Many politicians are still looking for greater military weaponry and action as the answer. Others are looking to help build the struggling nations to a higher standard of living. We must find a balance for survival that will bring peace on earth and good will toward men that we dream and sing about in our houses of worship.

We find now that the new spiritual thoughts coming forth are testing our beliefs for authenticity. We have clung too long to the beliefs of ancient days in gods and angels whereby all things were explained by the supernatural. But science has opened Pandora's Box of mysteries; it cannot be re-closed and pushed aside any longer. The portals of the heavens that had been such a mystery for so long by superstition and planned methodology has finally been opened so that we are now able to see a heavenly array of suns by the trillions, gathered in billions of spinning galaxies spreading out over trillions of *light years* of seemingly empty space. We are finding now that this "empty space" surrounding us is sprinkled with what they have termed Dark Matter, the very building blocks of new suns and planets.

Time itself has become completely incomprehensible, as the myth of a 6000-year-old earth has been lengthened to millions of years of formation before we even arrived in all our splendor. Archaeology has uncovered a past filled with life forms we never realized ever existed. So it is not a question of whether we believe these scientific facts or not; they are still facts that someday we all must face, even as we had to face the reality of the earth circling the sun as Galileo had proven some 600 years ago and the Roman Church scoffed at. The question before us now is whether we desire knowledge and new hope, or to cling to the ignorance of a fading, failing past. Each of us must help decide our future.

Suddenly, we can realize the insignificance of our earth as we find it to be only a minute blue speck tucked away in an arm of a rather insignificant galaxy in an ever-expanding, circling universe. It is no longer the motionless center of God's creation as taught by Aristotle nearly 2300 years ago and still held to be a truth in the religious world of Creationism. Instead, it is a tiny planet moving in its elliptical path around one of billions of suns in one of billions of galaxies in the vastness of space.

Where, then, do we look in this vastness of the universe for the Throne of God that has been created in our minds by our religious leaders? Our giant telescopes and listening devices have failed to discover even a minute trace of it. Our space probes have revealed nothing that resembles what we have been told. We are at a loss to know which way to turn as new revelations begin to unlock the mystery of creative life and finds us completely unprepared to face the new world that lies before us. This makes us realize that unless we have studied and measured and compared as our scientific efforts examine all theories, we can know very little of what we have been told and what we claim to believe. We are ignorant of the reality in which we live, fooled by the very ones we trust to guide us.

The door of the United States has long been opened to the world as the last bastion of individual freedoms that mankind has longed for. But even the formation of this bastion of freedom has been indelibly marked by the religious fanatical witch-hunts and the terrible, ungodly burning at the stake of the superstitiously condemned "witches" in our first colonies. Soon there came the trading in the inhuman slavery of others from the dark regions of Africa by the very ones who came to America for individual freedom, in life and in religion. It also brought the near genocide of the original race of people that greeted the White Man to this new land. America was really not the Land of the Free that we sing about in our schools and churches, for thousands were brought to our shores in chains for slaves of the landowners who were given grants of land by the European kings who claimed this New World, and bondage was given the original race who greeted us.

But slowly we are striving to right the many wrongs that haunt our past so that we can build anew.

A new race of people has been forming here in this last millennium as immigrants from the older, more stringent nations have inter-married and formed a mixture of blood-lines and cultures that will, in time we hope, put an end to the confusion of race and color. A "New American" is coming forth. Thomas Jefferson, one of the founders of our free nation, unknowingly helped in the mixing of bloodlines as has been revealed in these later years. Perhaps in time it will help us end the confusion of the many customs and religious beliefs that still separate us from one another. Just perhaps, also, it will help us understand another's point of view to help bring a new peace to our Land.

As we look at our present world at the beginning of this new era there are many reasons for us to have confidence of a bright and promising future. But we must also be very apprehensive. We can easily visualize the reality of a stark, frightening future that could be awaiting us. Bloodshed and suffering of the innocent abounds throughout the world as racial and religious wars still rage in country after country. The world's population is exploding, already at 6 billion as this millennium opens, creating problems we never dreamed of as we were building our great materialistic societies; problems such as starvation, homeless families, disease, clogged highways and byways, and crime hitting new highs.

Even our earth is dying because of the poisonous fumes that we have emitted so freely into the atmosphere. We have torn into her bosom for minerals and decimated her beautiful forests, leaving her naked to the destructive elements of wind and rain. National disasters of gigantic proportions have struck repeatedly and have laid smaller nations in a completely helpless condition, each with the death toll reaching into the thousands, and each crying out to us for help.

Both large and small nations continue to build their arsenals of war for their supposedly protection from one another. Utter destruction by nuclear and gas warfare hangs over us by a mere thread. Children shoot children in our schools. We pray for deliverance, and wait - in vain. The relief from this turmoil and nature's destructive forces is still not in sight as our prayers to our Heavenly Father go unanswered.

Somehow, man must learn that it is within himself to build the better world. The supernatural way does not exist. It never has. We cannot wait any longer for the prayers of our religious leaders to reach the nebulous portals of Heaven and save us.

Is this a doomsday scenario? Are we really creating a progressive society for the world as we so smugly seem to think? Or are we building for an Armageddon of a different type than what our religions has taught? Nihilism is growing as belief in governmental law and morality is tossed aside for individual law as expressed by the Law of the Gun. "Force must prevail." This is the belief; that conditions in our social order have become so bad that destruction of it seems more desirable than the constructive programs to relieve it. Revolutionary steps must be taken, we are told, even terrorism and assassinations of present leaders are a stark reality.

This is the Armageddon we are facing.

But is everything really so bad, or is our minds running away from reality? Are all life forms facing extinction as the earth turns into a stark, lifeless mass before our very eyes, such as the moon and the planet Mars, or is a new earth literally coming down from a new Heaven to save us as Isaiah visioned? (Isaiah 65:17). Was his vision only a myth we fail to understand?

13

Or will there finally be an awakening within us, a longing to turn us toward building that new and better way of life, a new era of peace on earth that man has dreamed of for many centuries? This certainly can be the reality we can hope for, if we realize that Change is coming, and that we must begin to vision what we truly desire for our world.

Isaiah saw such a possible change centuries ago. He wrote of it so that we might find hope, if we, too, will change our ways as he pleaded for his beloved Israel to do.

Yes, it could happen. The scenario can be as we desire it. It is entirely up to mankind, to each of us, to catch the dream of Brotherly Love that Jesus spoke of, and make it happen. Or we can continue blindly on the same merry-go-round of our lives as each of us strive individually to catch that golden ring of wealth and happiness that we have been reaching for down through time, as we cling desperately to outmoded religious myths handed to us for our salvation. We mock the scientific findings that could open our minds to a far greater understanding of the heavens, of our own planet and even of ourselves than the majority now possess. We hide smugly behind the veil of ignorance - and blind faith. On Sunday we pray for guidance, and we wait. Next Sunday we pray for guidance, and we wait again. This is the circle of life we live in.

It would be much wiser if the realization would come to each of us that a new age of awakening is here. It would reverse this seemingly inevitable thinking pattern we have today if we so desire it. We must first have the vision that a new and better world is a possibility. It cannot be a world for only a small minority as in the past, the "Have" against the "Have-not". It must be a national vision, even a worldly vision, a new hope given the people to strive for. Then, each of us must strive to build it in our own little kingdoms as we were admonished, "That ye love one another as I have loved you." This is the Golden rule, the diamond in the rough, and the Pearl of great price in all of creation. This is the Golden Grail that King Arthur sought - and failed to find. It is now our turn.

There are many who already have come to the realization that perhaps we are here for a definite, divine purpose; and that we may not be ruled by blind chance as so many believe. We also may not be as pawns to be divided in the seemingly game between God and Satan that has been taught for centuries by theology. Each of us has been given the traits and the talents needed for our place in society, and born unto the parents and into the environment for our schooling in this lifetime, and it is our will, whether strong or weak, that we must use to walk the path set before us.

This is the mystery of life that mankind has ignored through the centuries. But has the seeds of life been strewn willy-nilly into the world of nature's forms commonly called the "Garden of Sin", as we presume, to mature as the winds of chance and luck prevail? Or is it possible that each of us has our own little niche in the universe that we must develop as even the atoms in every body has their innate calling and duty to perform, slightly different in each body? For only in that manner can progress be achieved, and a better world become a reality. It takes the butcher, the baker and the candlestick maker so to speak, to make a society, and each job and position is needed, just as the heart and lungs is needed, but also are the arms needed - and the thumbs - for a well-working body.

Perhaps the temptations around us seem stronger than we can bear and we seemingly fail. But there are no failures; there are only changes in direction, a detour, or perhaps a pause. God is not mocked; He is not the looser that He is portrayed. It will be as it should be, no matter the time

15

involved, for the pendulum always swings back to balance. The revelation of a new world is beginning, and it will come; the time we know not.

Our prayers, "Thy kingdom come . . ." has been to no avail for 2000 years as we waited for the supernatural to happen.. It is time for us to examine our ways and build those new dreams for the future that we desire so that "Thy Kingdom" can come. We must add Inspiration and Aspiration to our thoughts and dreams, just as the gurus of "Get Rich" books and seminars teach, but it must be the thoughts and dreams of a new and better world for all.

-2-

The Awakening

Throughout every era of mankind's long struggle upward there has been those times when a nucleus of inquisitive minds began to feel an inner urge for a deeper knowledge and experience than that which had been given them by their leaders and teachers. These were the glorious times of which we have looked back upon in our long history and marveled at the knowledge possessed even then.

We study the Egyptian era with their colossal pyramids, their Goddesses who guided them, and the beginning of their priesthood. We study the Grecian era with the first of the great philosophers such as Socrates and Plato, and of course the first scientific minds of Thales, Pythagoras, and Aristotle. From there we are led to the Renaissance of Europe in the 17th and 18th centuries with the many great minds of that era. We are amazed at the wisdom of those great minds for these were not of the great religious world of Catholicism, but rather the thoughts of free-thinking men. All of these, and even many more if we delve deeper, brought mankind to a higher level of consciousness and a greater freedom of thought.

Now we find that same feeling of hunger for deeper knowledge flooding over the world, beginning with movements such as the Rosicrucians, Freemasonry, and the alchemists who hid their inner knowledge in rituals and magic. With these came the great inquisitive minds of Madame H.P. Blavatsky and Charles Darwin who opened the door to new theology. During the twentieth century just past science opened the door to a new and greater era. It was the realization of the true beginning of time and the discovery of the continual expansion of the universe, and, of course, we saw the beginning of the computer age. With these new discoveries coming forth we find a consuming desire for more and more knowledge of man himself.

A portion of this desire, quite surprising to most, is for an understanding of the esoteric, the mystic side of life instead of only the emotional experiences of ritual and dogma offered by the denominational world of religion. For instance, why are we here? Is there really a purpose in our life? Why are there the variances in birthrights, when we are told that, "All men are created equal"?

People are beginning to realize that there are many mysteries that mankind has never truly faced, buried instead by theologies and dogma down through the centuries to mesmerize and satisfy the masses. The ecstatic experiences of pomp and ritual for the senses instead of true knowledge for the soul had been substituted by the early Church for the true teachings of Jesus, offering them a "salvation" instead of a new and better way of life.

But now the time seems to have arrived for the unveiling of these mysteries that have lain hidden deep within the myths and legends of the ancient past. The stories and fables are still there for us to read, just as the parables of Jesus and his great and wonderful teachings of love and empathy for one another, but now the esoteric meanings are being revealed so that the beauty of the meaning of his teachings and of life itself can finally be realized.

There are countless mysteries about this life and this earth upon which we dwell that we have never imagined existed. Only a few, the Seekers, ever realize the answers. We seldom even question our beliefs as they are passed from generation to generation and accepted solely by faith in the vain promises held forth to the trusting masses. But these mysteries could very well be called the "who, what, why, when, and where" of life itself and are at the very heart of our existence. It is through questions such as these that we learn of the unknown and truly grow as a society.

These five rather small words when used for deeper knowledge begin unlocking the doors to revelations of the unknown worlds that few have realized existed around us and even within us. They include the World of Objective Thought, the conscious mind in which we truly dwell, the World of Subjective Thought which is the servant and creative factor, the "Doer" part of us, and the World of Desire out of which all things emanate. We are only aware of the World of the bodily form in which our soul is encased, but we find it to be the world governed by the law of entropy, short-lived and filled with our vanities. Only that few, the true seekers, ever realize the existence of the higher worlds in which Consciousness is the everlasting dweller. "Before Abraham was, (the form) I Am (the spirit)." The body dies and disintegrates back to dust, but Consciousness (the "I Am") is ageless.

But this consuming desire for the esoteric does not come to all at the same moment in life. There is an appointed time for each of us, a time of hesitation and a time for readiness. At some moment in our life we hear a "A knock" that comes through our intuition, perhaps an insight to a troubling thought that opens the door to a new revelation. Other times, one must sink to the lowest levels of living before the knock can be heard, before the reality that a more perfect way must exist. Then there are times, sad though it may be, that death overcomes the body before the knock can be answered and another lifetime of schooling is wasted. But we can be well assured that each and every one of us will have our Day of Learning and hear our "call to come Home", for we must believe that our God is fair and just with all His creation and not only for a chosen few as we have been taught by the example of Israel being "God's Chosen People", with all others to be destroyed. Truly this is a Judaic belief and not factual even though it is accepted as fact.

We find this time of awakening so true even with people who succumb to the faster paces of the life of power. Some turn to alcohol and drugs to keep up the fallacy of a happy and full life. Others finally realize the futility in their lives and strive to find a new and better concept.

But some do not respond in time and death ensues. The soul must then wait for another time for its karmic past to be balanced - and rest assured it will be. But this is another story waiting for its place and time to be revealed in later pages.

This is the lesson to be learned in the parable of the Prodigal Son who was led by his carnal desires until his sudden awakening to his wasted life of vanity. We must believe that this is not the story of only one son, but rather the story of all of humanity waiting its moment of realization. But it comes only when the mind has reached the level wherein a higher sense of reasoning and individual longing brings to mind the possibilities that could exist with a "New Birth" into a higher plane of existence. This is not waiting for "Pie in the sky" of our religious teachings, nor the guilt complex of the myth of "The fall of man" and our being born into sin, but it is the sudden realization that we must be here on earth for a purpose, and our life is the searching for The Way, filled with mistakes through our ignorance but awaiting the guidance by the Voice within and balanced through the experiences of life.

It is this insatiable quest for knowledge and the ability to reason that separates the Homo sapiens from the many other species that make up the world of form that we call life. Even in the family of mankind we find there are many races at many different levels of consciousness and understanding, and there are people in every race at different levels of knowledge. But we are finally coming to the realization that we are all of one specie to seek the same Path of fulfillment, each in our allotted time, and we must learn to "Love one another as I have loved you", and to help in time of need. "I was hungered, and ye gave me meat; I was thirsty, and ye gave me drink; I was a stranger, and ye took me in . . ." (Matthew 25:35). Our God has many faces and forms that we do not recognize as He".

First, there must come this awakening, this inspiration and desire for understanding.. We must hunger for a better Way. The desire must grow within us for a change of life until the vision of the Way clearly comes and the sudden realization of the possibilities that exist in each of our lives.

Thus begins the search and the aspiration for the deeper esoteric knowledge of why we are here and what the goal is that has been set before us. Think of all the self-help books and courses that have come forth in these later days to help us turn the corner of life, though few there are that have actually placed man as a part of the universal family of the Consciousness we call "God". Most teach of an individuality type of "success" instead of building a better society for all.

From the moment Homo "took of the fruit thereof and did eat" from the "Tree of the *knowledge of Good and Evil*" as spoken of in the myths of Genesis, "the eyes of both were opened, and they knew that they were naked. . ". Until then they were led by blind instinct as were all the animals, but the brain of that branch which became Homo Sapiens had at that time developed to the realization of consciousness, of being aware of being a separate entity. But he had nothing; no home for protection from danger and weather, no food, no clothing, no memory and no knowledge of anything. He was indeed naked of all things. He had to survive by his own efforts, "by the sweat of they face . .". Even the instincts of his past were overshadowed and dimmed by his awakened mind. Life no longer just came naturally.

From that very moment Homo became aware of "good and evil", or right and wrong,. "And the Lord God said, 'Behold, the man is become as one of us, to know good and evil . . '. From that moment man began the long search for knowledge and survival that is still going on, for we are still so very far from the glories that mankind can attain when he finally awakens.

So, today we find that same instinctive desire for a greater understanding still flowing over the land, stronger than ever. Of course, skepticism still abounds in much of the masses, and the "Prince of Darkness", the carnal mind of vanity, fights for its seat of power over the objective, thinking mind. We must always be aware that deception has been a ruling factor in our lives as we are continually bombarded by all manner of speeches and advertising, from health, medical claims, and even religions, through the gauntlet of human needs and desires, until we feel the inner spiritual aspirations for a new life. All manners of beliefs can be found, each claiming to be the Truth, so it is imperative that we choose carefully the path up the mountain that we will follow.

Many years ago P.T. Barium of the circus world stated it very bluntly in his remark that there is a sucker born every minute - and also someone who will fleece him. Our only hope for protection is our ability to reason and the admonition to "weigh all things; accept that which is good."

Gullibility, of course, is certainly not a trait that one desires. Yet, to be too skeptical and refuse all new ideas is nothing more than a closed mind that we have possessed for centuries on end. This trait makes progress very difficult. But such has been the manner as we read of the denial of the acceptance of scientific facts from their very beginning, from Copernicus and Galileo through Darwin, Einstein and Hubble, by the very religious world which supposedly should be teaching us the knowledge we need to grow.

This is the reason that rationality is such a very important trait for us to learn. It is the ability to weigh all things in the light of knowledge and reason, surmising perhaps a possibility might exist rather than the blind acceptance of the myriad of unproven theories and beliefs that have bombarded mankind these many centuries. The great gift of rationality was brought forth to us from ancient Greece as we were inspired by Plato to "Question all things; accept that which is good", and to "Know thyself. Presume not God to scan. The proper study is Man." This is what brought us the birth of the scientific world by Aristotle, Ptolemy, Galileo, and others through time, and which opened the closed doors of ignorance and skepticism with the freedom of thought and *the ability to prove all things.*

With these questions of why we are here and the accountability of all for the disobedience of one, it can readily bring another question to mind. Can this really be the plan of a just and loving Father/God who seemingly discriminates so unjustly against race and individuals? It seems rather plain that somewhere, sometime, and somehow a great misunderstanding has been allowed to take charge of the spiritual teachings of the masses as the priesthood took over for the voice of the Father within each of us.

We cannot accept that life is just a game of chance in birthright and birthplace, nor can we accept that it is governed so unfairly by some great supernatural power high in the heavens. The long string of DNA which forms our bodies within our mother's womb is our history, the blueprint of our generations from far in the past. But from where comes the Consciousness, the mind to control this body? This is the mystery we have not solved.

Immutable laws such as gravity and cohesion, light and darkness, heat and cold, govern the universe of which we are a part and has brought time and form from out of the Chaos of the beginning. There is also a law of Creativeness that has never been recognized in the atoms of every form, but hidden by our search for a deity in Heaven instead of recognizing the Creator within us as Jesus taught.

There was a beginning. Just as the myths of Genesis tells us, though the element of time and the procedure of creation differ by a few billion years with the Creationists 6000-year interpretation of the analogy in Genesis. This new understanding of the beginning has been a great stumbling block for the priesthood ever since it was introduced in the early twentieth century. But the time for the unveiling of the divine plan had not yet arrived for the masses. Its time is coming, though we do not know the day and the hour. It is awaiting the time when the people will reach the pinnacle of desire for knowledge of the spirituality of man within this material body.

The promise, "Seek and ye shall find" is only for those seeking truths instead of experiences. They are as Columbus was in 1492, leading the world to a new land. Can it still be another century or two away for the acceptance, with the ever-increasing suffering coming upon the world to balance the atrocities of yesteryears? Surely we hope that it cannot be that far off. But the signs of its coming are in the stars of the universe as we were told that it would be, and the longing is in the breast of the people waiting for it to arrive. The sun is even now beginning to enter the constellation of Aquarius to bring forth the new age.

Our goal here on this earth has never meant to be only the striving for satisfaction of our bodily senses and materialistic desires as we seemingly imagine. We must learn somehow that amassing gold and power over others is only a finite fantasy filled with traps to ensnare our mind. There can be a future far greater than we have ever imagined waiting to be visualized and brought forth into reality if we can raise our eyes and vision it. For, "Without a vision the people perish."

The theological concepts of religion have bound us to the dogma that it has expounded for centuries. We must free ourselves from the Gods of Baal and turn instead to the true teachings of Jesus and the voice within. It is time for us to read his words - and begin practicing what he teaches. Let us follow Jesus and not Simon Peter.

There has been a divine cohesion down through time, so that the great minds of the past, the shamans and the prophets, were allowed to "see" and dream of the future they visioned and were able to record these early bible stories in crude hieroglyphics that Apostle Paul called analogies. But these myths and legends became a religion by the priesthood who replaced the early mystics, but who failed to understand the true meanings, substituting them with literal interpretations and gods to care for and "save" the people.

But now there is more than just a small ray of hope of a better understanding. We have been blest with a free will and sound reasoning, and a faith in our abilities that makes every concept, every dream, a possibility. For more than 18 centuries the faith of the people was fastened upon the nebulous interpretations passed down from the theologies of the Roman Church as written down in the Nicean Creed of 372 A.D. under the direction of Emperor Constantine, binding the people with the threat of heresy and death. Later, the voices of philosophic prophets tried to show a better way during the days of the Renaissance, when Martin Luther broke the binders of the Church by his revelation of its devious practices.

Now, the vision of the dawning of a new day is again spreading through the hearts and minds of many as the pages of time flutter past. This time it is a scientific renaissance, and a spiritual vision that is being awakened, in place of another religious kingdom of materialistic vanities and experiences. There is the hope coming over the world of the final releasing of mankind from the vain thoughts that the materialistic world of power and greed is the true desire of the ego within us, and that God is separate from us, high in the heavens. A new realization is coming forth, a new vision of the possibilities that can be attained by a new way of thinking. We are finding that the secret of every new attainment begins with a thought and the desire, followed by action toward the goal.

It is not a path of spiritual *EXPERIENCES* through rituals and songfest that we seek. It is rather finding the path to the attainment of the Kingdom of God within, the peace and joy of living in a society built through works of love and charity, by our own actions and duties, and the realization of the oneness of all. The God on the heavenly throne is the myth we must face, placing the Throne within our own heads and breasts. It was only an allegory to bring us to the consciousness within to guide us as Jesus taught of the Father within, but we began worshipping the allegory instead of the Christ spirit that can flood through us as it did Jesus. The path of at-one-ment will lead us to the Holy Grail that has been sought even in stories since the days of King Arthur, but has never been found.

So, now is the time for us to search for the Way, not just pray for it to come. We have been told, "Faith without works is dead", and we can truly see the results all around us as our earth dies before our very eyes as we desperately cling to our faith.

There can be no other way. We have found that the twentieth century mind was slowly beginning to turn from the materialistic world of desires to the reality that all is truly vanity. Old ways and beliefs were slowly being shaken and a new light was beginning to shine as religion, modern philosophy and science began to join hands, as they surely should. This tide must continue.

Already, many good things are happening, bringing loving help to The needy and a feeling of joy to the doers. We can see that Brotherly

Love is beginning to flower as we reach out to help our neighbors and to build a better foundation of education and medical assistance for all. We are building homes for needy families. We are helping the homeless, the widows and the elderly. We are meeting the needs of nature's casualties, and many other acts of caring.

Yes, it is a slow process as we realize the need throughout the world. But it is the sign that the feminine, feeling part of Home Sapiens, separated so long when the masculine, warring part became the ruling priesthood far back in the Egyptian days and continued throughout these many centuries, but is now finally finding its way back into our hearts.

But the masculine energy that took over religion and the control of the masses and raised its own phallic spires toward the heavens will not step aside nor join in this change. The Klu Klux Klan of the religious South was turned into this bigotry and hatred toward those who were different. Even now we see the picking up of weaponry and the banding together in private militias to "protect their rights". We find them killing doctors who perform abortions. We see them blowing up the offices to prove their point. This, of course, is nothing more than the carnal mind holding to its desires of individualistic power rather than building a new and better world through love and understanding.

Time, we hope, will be on our side as we strive to turn the corner toward this dream of the Kingdom of God here on earth. But our teachings and our present way of life must be challenged more and mankind as a whole must be shown this new vision of what life really could be if we would only try a little harder. It must begin to be taught in our schools. It must be taught from the pulpit instead of songfest and loud, lengthy prayers. Emphasis must be upon the duty and the ability to train the children we have been given in a home life of love and devotion, and the "why" of our existence - when we, too, finally learn it.

Our leaders must turn from their political haggling and mythical teachings to the vision of what it requires to build a better world for all, not just for the "Chosen few" as we have today, but better for all the world. At the present time they have lost the vision of "A government of the people, by the people and for the people" that our founding Fathers visualized for this new nation. They have given us instead a fictitious hope of a crowning glory in a nebulous Heaven - if we will only believe their story and pay our tithes.

The scribes are already busily writing the epitaph for this passing era. Perhaps it will be as the blind men who described the elephant as each felt of the different areas of its body, the trunk, the ear, the tail, and its feet. Each scribe will contain that portion of the truth that conveys his perspective. Some will bring forth the glorious opportunities of amassing extreme wealth. Others will write of the Grapes of Wrath midst a land of plenty. Others will see the beginning of anarchy as the terror organizations infiltrate fertile minds as their brand of individualism tears at the very roots of our society.

All the scribes will be correct in a sense. The signs are there for each of these ways. But he who writes of the time of the greatest awakening that the earth has ever known, both scientifically and spiritually, will bring forth a greater truth and hope than all the rest. We have already reached a pinnacle never before dreamed of in materialistic achievements. The time is here, now, for us to begin bringing forth that new world of love and hope as envisioned by the prophets of bygone eras as knowledge brings us the realization of the possibilities that are still within us,

Raymond Moyer

As we have been told, there is a time for everything; a time for planting and a time for harvest, a time of darkness and a time for light. The veil of darkness has been rent by the vanguard of souls before us who "saw" the light of a new day, and it is our duty to bring it forth.

This new spiritual awakening is on the horizon. It cannot be denied any longer, or darkness will again fall over our land as the dark ages fell over Europe a few centuries ago.

-3-

A New Awakening

As the world reached the middle of the twentieth century a new voice was heard "crying in the wilderness". At first it was ignored as we do a crying child tugging at our side, hoping that it would subside by inattention. But as we finally and impatiently listened, we heard the shocking, almost unbelievable words, "God is dead! God is dead!"

It came from the mouths of our youth, those young men and women who would soon be replacing us in the business world and in politics. We were witnessing their reaction as they began to awaken to the realization that a change was needed in our way of life.

Looking back at those days that are still referred to as "The Turbulent Sixties" we now see them as a time when the young, growing minds that were filling our colleges pioneered a new freedom of their own. It was as if Plato once again stood before them in his flowing white robe with outstretched arms admonishing them to think and to reason for themselves.

"An unexamined life is a wasted life. Know thyself. Presume not God to scan. The proper study is man".

Plato could well have been teaching them the wisdom to question all things, and to reason through fact and intellect. For truly the time had come for man to begin thinking and reasoning for himself instead of continuing to be led blindly down the pathway of life by self-appointed leaders who knew only the dogma of their religion that was taught to them. We see that era of the Sixties now as a time when nearly all of the young generation began questioning age-old concepts of thought and family structure. They flagrantly cast aside the teachings of home and establishment, proclaiming the initial breakdown of the very foundation of our nation and our beliefs in God. Suddenly, our old familiar standards of life, liberty and the pursuit of happiness were being threatened by a lifestyle of freedom of standards, and marijuana became the preferred tobacco for smoking.

It was indeed a turning point in the American dream. The expansion of a higher level of education than ever before was made possible by the G.I. Bill to the mass of returning soldiers earlier in the late forties and fifties. Another war had even been fought, in Korea. Another was beginning in Vietnam. Now it was the children of these soldiers of World War II who were benefiting from a higher level of education to gain a new concept of life. With the underlying condition of society at that precise time, these young minds began forming a new future through the freedom of thought.

It was a very trying time for our nation, both for the young and for the parents who could not understand what was taking place. Throughout time it had always been the unwritten but dominant principal that the siblings follow the patterns and beliefs of the parents with little question. Now, suddenly, a revolution was erupting that was to tear asunder the very basics of our traditions.

The memory is still there of the riots at Berkeley College in California and the tragedy at Kent State in Ohio where rioting students were shot down by the militia.. Too many of the young were only restless and headstrong, and filled with the urge to be free before they learned the underlying responsibility it ensued. Thousands of runaways, many barely in their teens, filled the streets of San Francisco and Los Angeles and many other cities as they chased their rainbows and the elusive pot of nebulous gold.

The memory is also still vivid in many minds even yet of the great love-in and pot-smoking event called Woodstock, where the young tried to find solace and thrills in their newly found freedom and in one another. It has been rekindled in many minds by reunions years later by those who lived this phenomenon, as if to revive the days of their youth and their young glory. But times can never be brought back; they can only be remembered and imitated while the receding hairlines remain as a stark reality of the passing of time.

Crusades became the "in" thing in that era. Instilled by self-appointed leaders that always arise and are eager to step into the limelight to expound their radical thoughts and urge the unsuspecting followers onward, these crusades led to many crimes under the banner of a new kind of justice. They robbed banks for the money to carry on what turned into rampages of uncontrolled anger. People were killed during those crimes but that was the price that had to be paid, they reasoned.

We were very close to the beginning stages of anarchy as we watched helplessly on our televisions the looting and burning of our cities by the roving bands of uncontrolled youths. Much of Detroit literally went up in flames. Few were blamed. The day of the gun mania was beginning to dawn for it was another sign of individual power.

These were the first signs of anarchy that had ever flowed over our land of freedom. But the great cause was missing, such as the cry of freedom issued from our first colonies, or the Russian rebellion of the early part of the century that cried for freedom from oppression. Now it was only a cry for uncontrolled freedom, fueled by ambitious, self-appointed, immature, gloating leaders.

With this movement came the sudden attraction for the drum and guitar to give this explosive energy a new way of expression. The deep tones of the reverberating "beat" music was born while the words in their hearts were sung out in defiant voices. Out of this, of course, came very rich dissenters as their songs and music were published by the very establishment of which they sang against.

These were the ones the newspapers and television focused our eyes upon. These were the runaways and the defiant ones who believed in their total freedom to the very edge. These were the ones who filled our society with their free-sex living and their marijuana that led many on into the hard drugs that is the great destroyer of minds and lives. These were the ones that made the headlines glorifying the leaders that spurred the masses even farther.

Out of this also came the Gay movement in all its defiance. There had always been Gays, by another name of course, but now came the flaunting of it as an accepted way of life. Very soon another killer disease was thrust

34

upon us that struck down even the innocent that were caught by infusions of the tainted blood being sold for the purchase of more drugs. It turned into a slow, painful death and sorrow for all while the word "Aids" no longer meant helping others, but turned rather to the mark of a homosexual or drug lifestyle.

It was not the lifestyle that was the real problem, however. It was the arrogance of flaunting it as a normal way of life and the insisting of it being accepted as such. But America was not ready for such a change in the fleeting time that was expected and it did nothing but bring sorrow and pain and division to the very ones that it was meant to bring together.

There were other groups that also came forth in this era. Some of these were also defiant. But they were defiant only of being asked to fight another useless war in a far-off country called Vietnam. There had not been enough time to forget the no-win struggle in Korea, and this was to be no different.

For the first time in our history the young rebelled against being pawns in a national power struggle with no true meaningful mission to be accomplished. The colleges filled to capacity with very studious dissenters for as many years as were possible for the protection it offered from the draft. Others joined the national Guard of their states, to guard our homeland from any North Vietnam threat of invasion. Some even learned to fly the speedy jets.

But many were not so lucky. These were the ones that were forced to drift northward and disappear into the fastness of Canada, many never to be seen again by their grieving parents. They were forced from their own country because of their desire and belief of freedom of choice, the very cornerstone of our Constitution.

35

But far too many of the youths of this era tried to find their "Nirvana" in drugs, free-sex living and hard Rock music. It wasn't there to be found. These are the ones that had never caught the vision of a better world. They desired only their uncontrolled freedom to do as they pleased.

Many lives and families were ruined as these young lives searched in vain for their fantasies while their newly found freedoms became their demise. They filled the streets and highways as they strummed their guitars and sang their songs of defiance about the very Establishment that gave them the freedom to do it. They didn't build dreams; they only sang about them.

But there was still another group that came forth out of these times, a more quiet, seeking group. With it came the awareness that a new age was dawning. It was barely noticed until the shocking, powerful musical brought us the haunting song, "Age of Aquarius", and we began hearing of this new era that was just over the horizon. It was an age of promised hope that the bible had prophesied would come, though little was taught of it in the churches they had attended. They were taught only of "Pie in the sky" and ecstatic experiences here on earth through ritual and songfest.. This was the group that turned away en masse from the idle preaching of God and His wonderful love while He threatened His creation with eternal fire. They began searching for answers to the questions that that had always been ignored, questions that man had been asking for eons of time but the leaders could never answer.

These were the ones that listened intently to the faint, distant voice of Plato reaching across time. They head the voice of Buddha. They began to wonder, "What is the meaning of life? Why are we here? Where did we come from to be born on this small, insignificant planet? Are we here for only a short lifetime for no apparent reason and then just vanish into the fading past to await Judgment Day? What is death? Is it the end of all things for us?"

Most important of all was the question, "What is this great mystery called God?" No one was able to answer them. There was rhetoric. There was the offer of salvation for a nebulous "Home in Heaven" for only believing - and attending Church. But there were no answers.

The age of reasoning had arrived for these young souls as they weighed the teachings of the God of the heavens against reality of life. This was the beginning of the turning away from the authoritative church world and the beginning of searching for truths for a new day.

They found that Jesus taught of the God within. Even as in His day those that followed Him failed to understand The True Path. The Apostles looked for a Judaic Messiah for the salvation of their nation, not a new religion and a new way of life as He taught.

"Wilt thou at this time restore again the kingdom to Israel?" This was their last question to Him.

We have been given this same vision of a coming Messiah, with the return of Jesus, and find ourselves in this 21st century still looking for salvation from an exterior God who sacrificed himself for us. But the eyes and minds of many are beginning to be opened by a new vision. It is the vision of the True Path up the mountain, long covered by the brambles of dogma and the detours carved by theology. But the footprints of Jesus are still vaguely discernable if we truly seek for them.

"Pick up thy cross and follow Me," His words still beckon us. And He shows us that the Life of Love is still the Way.

It is not a Path that one accepts by faith. It is of Doing. Jesus and Guatama the Buddha spent many years in finding it. Both were tempted with power and riches to capitalize upon it. But each learned it by seeking. They gave their message freely, but only to those who hungered for it. To the others it was in parables.

There are many that are now asking the same questions that have never been answered. Where does the answers lie? We are admonished, "Ask, and it shall be given you; Seek, and ye shall find; knock, and it shall be opened unto you". There is also an oath given us: "For every one that asketh receiveth; and he that seeketh findeth; and to him that knocketh it shall be opened". It is the duty for each of us to seek the answers for ourselves by contemplation and reasoning. The day of meditation and higher thoughts is here.

Changes are coming. The Sixties opened the door to a new freedom of thinking and reasoning. Our future depends upon whether we can pick up the fallen torch and march to the music of another drummer, the God within each of us.

It takes a lot of courage and desire to change. It also takes Love of one another to make it a reality.

-4-

The Search for Truths

The outcry of the young Flower Children of the Turbulent 60's was not understood as a wake-up call by the sleeping, religious Establishment. To them it was only uncontrolled heresy, almost comparable to the dark days of the Inquisitions in early Europe. God's great plan was not to be questioned nor rebuked, the religious leaders cried out as they authoritatively thumped their bibles and raised them high overhead. It must be accepted by faith and love, for the Church was the Voice of God to the people, infallible.

It was those many unanswered questions, however, that made these young cry out in futility, "God is dead!" To them it was a truth. The God of their fathers of which they had been taught failed to hear their cries for help in their time of need. They had been taught to pray for answers. They prayed. But no answers came. So they cried out in anguish, "God is dead!"

This movement was the beginning of a new awareness of age-old teachings. Beneath it all was a new spiritual awakening as other religions were studied. It must be realized that nearly all religions had their beginning in the middle and Far Eastern countries that has been called the birthplace of civilization. The teachings of Tao of China, the Vedas of India, Zoroasterism of Persia, Jehovah of the Hebrews, all of these were searched by these young for a deeper understanding.

Yoga became a way of life for many, both for health and for spiritual growth as the pages of the Hindu Bhagavad Gita suddenly became opened to them. No longer were they reading the myths and legends of a supposedly chosen people who continually erred, but they were now reading the teachings that could well have been spoken by Jesus of Nazareth. Only the name of the deities were different. But what, really, is in a name in a different tongue except that it is a symbol of the same concept.

Of course there were those who followed self-appointed gurus that proclaimed themselves God Incarnates and led them into forms of so-called worship that was nothing more than the same mind control over the masses that they had left. They chanted and gyrated into trances, hoping to find the God Consciousness the gurus told them about. But they found only disappointment and very rich gurus. But these were the ones looking for an easier way to the Path without the individual seeking for the revelation to themselves.

But the true seekers found a new understanding of the old mysteries that preceded even the days of Jesus but proclaimed that which the Master taught His disciples in secret. The bible became a new book of understanding, in many cases in consort with the Bagavad Gita of India.

The legends of Adam, of Noah, of Abraham and of Moses became the legends of man's groping struggle upward. The age-old Vedas of India revealed a new concept of man and the inner spirit within to guide him. Soon it was realized that within all the religions of the world came the revelation of the oneness of creation. Only the words of the stories were different.

The Eastern teachings, however, were not found to be the sole answer to the western way of life. Not completely at least. Many of the truths can be applied and absorbed into our ways, but our whole manner of living is far different from the life of complete separation for a feeling of spiritual freedom as was interpreted. Through misunderstanding of their early teachers even as in the case of the western world, these eastern countries have misconstrued the teachings and adopted a belief of complete suppression of desire.

They failed to realize that desire was given us for a reason, to guide us to accomplishment. It is the very foundation of evolving upward. Their religions and beliefs turned them away from the age-old teachings of the mystic minds of yesteryears and we see them now wallowing in utter poverty and death as they cling to their beliefs of mind and body control, forsaking that part which teaches that performance of one's duties is the True sacrifice to God.

"Not by merely abstaining from work can one achieve freedom from reaction, nor by renunciation alone can one attain perfection. Perform your prescribed duties, which is better than not working, for a man cannot maintain his body without work. But perform these duties for Krishna (God)".

Thus saith their Bhagavad Gita. Thus also saith the bible, though in slightly different words in Ecclesiastes 9:10.

Out of this searching, however, came the discovery of the schools of metaphysics whose teachings reach far back into the days of the founding of all religions. Some of them still contain the teachings that Jesus and Plato and countless other great minds found in the mystery schools of Alexandria, Egypt centuries ago.

Of course such words as "mystery schools" frightens many, and it is taught through ignorance of their contents that they are the schools of the Devil. The dictionary states, however, that the word "mystery" means only a truth unknowable except by divine revelation.

Apostle Paul had admonished Timothy, "Great is the mystery of Godliness". He warned his disciples to protect the deeper truths from the wolves that he knew would come, but it was never completely revealed what those deeper truths were. Nor were the teachings of Jesus to His Inner Circle ever recorded. It is not surprising then, that these mystery schools have had to exist in a hidden world and have survived down through these many centuries of darkness to be given in this day to those who truly hunger for light.

Now we are hearing again of these mysteries of the kingdom of God and the relation between man and the great Universal Sea of Intelligence which man worships as a Deity. It is a far cry from the orthodox teachings of modern Christianity of fallen man and the grace of the offered salvation to those who believe the story.

What does these new teachings consist of that makes them more acceptable than that taught by the churches in which they had grown up? It is the sudden realization that man is far more than this body that we are encased in, but rather three-fold. "God" is a far cry from the anthropomorphic BEING seated high on a throne in the heavens above us while His angels write our epitaphs for Judgment Day. It is the mystery of the upward striving of the eternal life-force through the myriad of forms it has taken to become useful kinetic energy for creation.

People are realizing that this body is of the earth, earthy, formed from a seed, is born, matures, grows old and dies, and returns to the earth from which it came. This body does not evolve; it returns to its simpler forms of liquid and solid atoms. It is a form, a vehicle that this Conscious Self, this consciousness of being "I" that permeates this body, can use to learn how to express itself in the manner willed by the spiritual Father within.

Such did the Conscious Self within the body of Jesus learn so that the Christ Spirit could be revealed through him. We reiterate, "He learned obedience through the things that He suffered." Jesus was our example, our elder brother who admonished us "To pick up thy cross and follow me." We realize that each of us has our Cross to bear, just as He did.

It is the consensus of Theology that a new soul is brought into being at every birth, born into the sin of Adam, lives for a time as it is supposedly given the opportunity to accept Jesus as its Savior for being born, and at death it dies. At some future time its earthly body will be brought back to existence in a miraculously and simultaneously manner for this short-lived soul to re-enter for judgment of its earthly actions, then to be rewarded or sentenced as the case may be. This supposedly is what "The restoration of all things" is taught to be.

Such a belief is now being questioned by this awakened and reasoning group. They have found that the body is not something that just miraculously happens and has no history. We know that each body is linked with its past generations by the DNA of the father and the RNA of the mother. From this pattern in the seed a new earthly form is created, and its genes can be traced back through the family tree from which it came.

Biblically this is shown in the genealogy of Jesus as it traces His body back to the House of David, showing that indeed Joseph was his earthly father. If not, the genealogy as shown in two books of the bible is false.

But what of the consciousness within, the soul, that spark of awareness of being a separate entity? Has it no past, no generations to show its upward progress? Yet, it has instincts dating back to ancient times. This is the real "I", the "I Am" which Moses discovered "high upon the mountain". The body is only a vehicle for its use to manifest and that disintegrates at death.

From whence, then, did this soul come to enter the earthly body? Just how were the parents chosen? We can readily see that discrepancies exist that show we are not born on equal levels as we are taught. How is this explained? What happens to our soul after the death of the body as it waits for its call to justice?

Theology has no answer. Though the body which is only a finite nature, an earthy vehicle, has a history, it is claimed that the soul, really a spark of the Infinite, has none. Each soul is claimed to be a new creation at birth. Deep within metaphysics and the ancient writings, however, a possibility has been found.

"Never was there a time when I did not exist, or you, or all of the kings. Nor in the future shall any of us cease to be. As the embodied soul continuously passes, in this body, from boyhood to youth and on to old age, the soul similarly passes from one body into another body at the death of its present one, in its appointed time."

"The self-realized soul is not bewildered by such a change; it knows that It is an eternal part of the Absolute. For that which pervades the entire body is indestructible. No one is able to destroy the imperishable soul. Only the material body of the eternal Living Entity is subject to destruction and change. For the soul there is no birth nor death. Nor, having once been, does it ever cease to be. It is unborn, eternal, undying, and primeval. It is not slain when the body is slain."

Do these words contradict the teachings of Jesus? Was this a new teaching? It is folly to think that the Hebrew writings were the only true words of wisdom regarding the Supreme. The reply must, therefore, be with an emphatic "NO" to the questions above about contradiction and new teachings.

Did not Jesus reveal to His followers that the spirit entities of Abraham and Moses were not dead with their bodies, but only in a different environment or world? Did He not say that the spirit that had lived before in the body of Elias had returned in a new body called John the Baptist?

He tried to teach that there was no death but only a change to a different world. Man has called this change for his soul as "death", an end. But the soul is spirit, unending. This is the new awakening that man is receiving, giving a new hope in a dying world.

We realize that there are as many interpretations of the scriptures as there are people, and the original speakers and writers have long departed. It is also a well-known fact that many of the scriptures have been grossly mis-translated due to the later misunderstanding of the minds that initially wrote the letters, and also to conform to the thinking of the translators.

We are finding that accepting by faith the teachings that have been handed down through the Roman Church is fading. Five hundred years ago people were ordered by the Church to "believe by faith" that the world was flat and that the sun and the planets revolved around the earth as Aristotle had proclaimed. Millions of people were killed in insufferable ways for believing differently. But faith in this teaching did not make it so.

In the past our religions were our comfort. It told us of a God in Heaven, how He formed the earth and its inhabitants as the center of the universe only 6000 yeas ago, and that we had a home with Him when we die.

Not content in these whims and practices of the past, the minds of many are finding the folly of continuing to follow these concepts of yesteryears and are probing the secrets that science and psychology are uncovering for a broader understanding. Sadly, the greater portion of the masses is still content to be led, creating the opportunity for leaders to form their dynasties and hold back new revelations as they come forth.

It is this greater portion of mankind that still demand by their very actions the laws and constraints that strive to mold our lives and societies into patterns of moral behavior. It is claimed that without these constraints we would have anarchy as Individualism would certainly take over. But those who have learned to live by the love of all things can live without them. Individualism has already taken over.

It is the philosophy of the life that we choose that can build the better society we long for. Until we learn how to accept that philosophy of divine guidance through our intuition, our Father within, we must have the Law of man to guide us.

To become a philosophy of life a thought or concept must become a rational and reasonable enough idea to be accepted by enough people. This, of course, does not guarantee the truth of the concept, but only its acceptability and rationality for belief.

As William James, a noted Philosopher of the past, stated in an effort to clarify the relation to truth, "You can say of an idea either that it is useful because it is true, or that it is true because it is useful. Both ideas mean the same." It does not state, however, that either is true.

This brings to mind the rationality of human nature and its capacity for what is termed "Faith". This is the ability to believe above all else and the willingness to act upon this belief, even though doubt is still possible. This leaves Truth as a nebulous thought and dependent upon the rationality and philosophy of life in one's mind. This nebulous thought is true or not as based upon one's belief, but true only to the believer.

This is the rationality that has formed our religions in the past in an effort to explain the immutable powers and laws of the universe. Only by the creation of a Supernatural Entity could these be explained and believed, but without the tested proof that is needed.

Certainly there can be little wonder that these younger, inquisitive minds of the early 60's would begin to question the claim that such a theology as taught could be God's Holy Word, and that such an organization of the Medieval Church with its bloody history could be the mediator between God and man. They had entered into the Age of Reasoning through greater knowledge. They had realized that Religion is, in a sense, only a branch of Philosophy and psychology, the studies of the powers of man in the universe as he strives to understand his place in the great, overwhelming puzzle of life. But it is based upon faith and emotions alone.

The door to spiritual understanding is being opened for us. The search has only begun. We realize that cults will come and go as they have in the past, as long as people will follow blindly "By faith" the self-appointed leaders that eagerly step forth and offer their outstretched coffers.

Understanding and Truth are not gained by this method. It comes only to those who seek it. It cannot be purchased by tithes and prayers of the Fathers. Anything that separates us from one another by race, by color, by creed, by belief, or by leaders whether Democratic, Republican, Catholic, Protestant, or Muslim cannot be Truth.

Perhaps the Age of Aquarius is just another dream of man. He has dreamed of many things down through time as he envisioned the Promise of "a new heaven and a new earth". Through these dreams and desires he has evolved to today's world. But the true world of reality for our soul is the infinite world of thought and Spirit as the Adepts have claimed and the finite world that we know is a horrible, suffering exercise and example to awaken us out of our apathy.

Life is too short for this to be all there is for mankind.

-5-

The Meaning of Religion

As we speak of a new way of life and the renewing of our minds, we should strive to understand exactly what is meant. That is why the absolute meaning of words is one of the most important tools for a complete and clear understanding of a subject and even of one another. Words can have different meanings in different languages and cultures so that a perfect translation can be a difficult problem. Words even change their meaning over time and usage. This is the problem that we should be aware of as we search for a better understanding of what we call our religion.

It would be proper, then if we would strive to find the true meaning of what is meant by the word, "religion" and analyze it, for it truly is an important part of life and future. As we enter the 21st century it is time for us to begin finding and using the knowledge that is available for us to create a far better world, both materialistic and spiritual, than we have in the here and now.

The Standard American Heritage dictionary states that Religion is: 1. (a): "A personal or institutional belief in and reverence for a supernatural power or powers regarded as creator and governor of the universe". (b): "A personal or institutional system grounded in such a belief and worship."

What, then, is meant by the term, "supernatural power"? Let us again look for a meaning of the words so that we can be truly sure of that which we speak.

Supernatural means, (1) "Powers or abilities above or beyond what is natural, transcending the ordinary course of nature, and attributed to a power that SEEMS to violate or go beyond natural forces to attain its ends."

There is one more meaning that we must examine, from the same dictionary, for it, too, applies. It is, (2): A set of beliefs, values, and practices based upon the teachings of a spiritual leader".

With these explanations we can begin to understand the basis of our religious beliefs. They are the beliefs in and reverence we have formed for a power or powers regarded as creator and governor of the universe, whose abilities, according to our understanding of them, SEEMS to violate or transcend natural forces to attain its ends, based upon the teachings and practices of our spiritual leaders.

It is difficult for us to realize the important position that religion has had upon the development of mankind down through the centuries. It has been the most universal activity of the human mind throughout the many races and is a symbol of the age-old mysteries that we have been taught since childhood. We were never really given a choice from which we could choose, but rather were taught the religion of our parents. In the Christian world it is the belief in the death of Jesus for the salvation of mankind, and his return to gather the faithful believers around him for their heavenly reward of eternal life.

For centuries this was basically the only choice, for knowledge was limited to what the Church offered or be branded as heretics. Its iron rule over even the beliefs of the people and giving no choice except the Nicene Creed and its proclamation of Christianity. But with such minds as Dr. Carl Jung, Charles Darwin, Edwin Hubble, Alfred Einstein, and the countless numbers of great inquiring minds, the veil has been lifted through the studies of psychology and the many branches of science to open a broader understanding of man and the universe.

Through the studies of Dr. Jung we have come to the knowledge that there is an inner "mind" within us, that which he called the psyche. Doctor Freud termed it the "Id", but both recognized the basic and primitive tendencies of an inner mind. Man became more than just body, but rather mind, knowing both good and evil, and able to create the world of his own vision. Today, because of these studies we have the world in which we live, and the teachings of the two classifications of our minds. These are the objective (the conscious) and subjective (the unconscious) that we have used down through time to visualize and create our own worlds, according to the desires that we have developed.

Religion, however, became the phenomenon down through time that engulfed the masses. It is an "object of perception", a dominant idea fed into the conscious mind that becomes a controlling factor in our emotional beliefs of a creator separate from man, though not something measurable and provable. It has relieved our minds of the creating ability that our minds really has, to build a better world which we can envision.

Many times as we have read stories in the bible we come upon a happening that we term as supernatural. The sudden creation of heaven and the earth, for instance, with its inhabitants as told in the first verses in Genesis. We have Noah building a huge ark - with only stone tools to work with. We have the parting of the Red Sea for Moses and nearly a million Israelites. We have also the sun standing still while Joshua won his battle. These we call the supernatural works of God in showing us His mighty abilities. But when we truly analyze these happenings, we find that superstition has been the guiding factor in the formation of these legends. Later, spiritual leaders have stood up and mesmerized the masses with a literal meaning of these analogies and into the belief in the "supernatural powers" of a mysterious, unknown Spirit BEING, separate from us in the heavens, because they cannot explain it in any other way.

But universal laws are never broken. The supernatural does not happen. They only SEEM to happen because of misunderstanding and seemingly no literal interpretation; the cause of what transpired was beyond our meager understanding. But there is a cause for every happening, and though we don't quite understand the circumstances - or the happening itself - does not make it a supernatural happening by a supernatural power.

But this is how we have been misled in the formation of our religions. Now, in this new time of awakening is the opportunity for us to broaden our outlook of life and realize the greatness and the vastness of all of creation throughout the universe, even the billions of blazing suns, all formed within the laws of gravity and cohesion. There is a scientific, factual explanation of the beginning of time, some 13-15 billion years ago. There has been the constant evolving of life on this tiny planet in the last million or so years of its existence. Now, in this 21st century is the time for us to use our god-given powers of reasoning for a richer and fuller understanding of what has been revealed through scientific and philosophical studies.

As we study the past and the religions that has been formed down through this long history of time we should always lovingly remember the uncounted number of truly faithful believers who have helped shape the societies we have today. We commend and love each for the faith and devotion they have brought to our world, and the love they have inspired in countless lives. We refrain with all of our self-control from being guilty of any disrespect or cruelty of words toward any, for satisfaction and sincerity of belief is the inalienable right promised to all. We must cherish this right for everyone, always remembering that argument and faultfinding of others is for the foolish.

All of these devoted people have not been remembered in our history as well they should have been. All were not sainted, for that is basically the custom of the Roman Church. Perhaps all should have been remembered in some manner for millions have given their lives rather than recant their faith and devotion, and millions more have set the examples along the way to lead others to a better life and a higher society. These exemplary lives of so many have shown the sincerity of the great and abiding faith that has shined forth through the many dark hours that our world has been subjected. Their belief was more than a religion; it was their very way of life, always striving to lift the mind and desires to a higher level of attainment in following the Path as they understood it. To each this devotion to their understanding will account for righteousness far more than dogma, even as Abraham's faith was accounted as righteousness.

They have been the cornerstone in creating a better world by their examples, even though it still is not the perfection as Apostle Paul had admonished us to strive for. "Be ye therefore perfect, even as your Father in heaven is perfect". We recognize and commend each and every one of these devoted people, realizing that no matter the creed that was professed, and even professed in the present day believers, there has been an inner light that far surpasses dogma. That light, the Christ spirit within each has been a guiding light in their living. Creed and belief has been secondary.

We of today can hardly imagine the faith deep inside the souls of the tiny ship Mayflower and the many other ships that brought the first settlers to the shores of America as they searched for the Promised Land of "Milk and honey". They were shown the vision of a new land filled with opportunities, and their faith made it a reality. There were also those that crossed the prairie lands of our nation following the vision they were given. This shows that faith can indeed move mountains - if the vision is bright enough, and the desire for it strong enough.

It is not creed or belief that brings these material things to reality. It is the physical building of the archetype that one visions in his mind. Even as the vision of a building from out of the mind of the architect comes to reality through action in the same manner. First comes the thought, then desire, and our actions bring forth the material form. There is nothing supernatural. It is the lawful pattern of creation.

It is well that we realize that each of us is in a level of understanding much the same as the grades of education. We will remain in that grade until we ourselves seek a higher level of understanding. We can remain in that grade as long as we are satisfied with the same knowledge, the same teaching, the same lessons of life, and refuse to climb upward to higher realms of thought and understanding. First we must have the vision. Then comes the desire, followed by the action to create the visual pattern.

Each of us must recognize that the time for inner growth is when we hear that wee small voice knock on the door of our intuition, telling us that something is not right, or a new realization comes to mind, and each must decide whether to open the door and let it in.

This urge of seeking knowledge has brought forth the great schools of learning that have arisen throughout the world. We read of the great library of Alexandra, Egypt centuries ago, the schools of the Rosicrucians and the Masons in the past centuries and also the hidden schools of the mystics showing us of today that there has been within man the yearning for a deeper feeling of the spiritual part, the unknown, that still remains unfilled. Thus we have psychology coming forth to lead us to the study of man himself, and that portion of the mind that is still unknown, the psyche.

The kindergarten of life is definitely full; in fact, it is overflowing. The masses seemingly are content to hear the same stories, the same promises, and the same message over and over, and this "milk" is what they are given. But one cannot grow and mature on milk alone. You must have meat. This is what Jesus added to the people's diet that followed him, It was not the fatted calf nor the meat of the bull. It was the meat of the fishes, or the message for the Pisces era which was dawning at the time. The day of the Law was ending and the new Commandment for this new day was "That ye love one another."

There are some, however, that are beginning to feel the need to move upward in spiritual knowledge beyond the realm of the illusion of individualism. We cannot continue hearing the profound statement that the earth is only 6000-7000 years old, and that man was supernaturally made complete in the twinkling of an eye. We cannot continue hearing the falsehood of the curse put upon man because of the "fall" and curse put upon "Adam". The time has come for these myths, these analogies as Apostle Paul called them, to be revealed in their true light and God's people released from the bondage of these old superstitions.

It is these restless ones who are bringing this new age of awakening to a reality as they cast aside the fears of doubt and begin questioning the teachings of this religious dogma that no longer applies to this dispensation. The day of the myth has passed; the day of understanding these myths is here, now.

There also has been in these past times many very devoted and god-fearing leaders caring for their flocks and feeding them very earnestly the plan of salvation as taught them in the schools of theology of their denomination, and believing it so earnestly. We commend them equitably as high for their devotion. Theirs has been the great responsibility of striving faithfully to guide their sheep toward the green pastures of heaven as they were trained, giving them a ray of hope for life eternal.

The sheep, in turn, look for their spiritual food in the guidance given them, and accepting the milk which is within their group understanding. Sadly, however, these sheep cannot survive on the amount of sustenance this food contains, totally dependent upon the knowledge the leader has. It is very apparent, then, that the responsibility of leading others is a grave undertaking. But devotion and faith in a belief and sincerity in the message does not in any manner attest to the truth of the teaching. It speaks only of the faith and sincerity that one has in the doctrine one has been given to teach others.

Sadly, however, we must point out that devotion, faith and sincerity has never been the sole requirements for spiritual leadership. Leadership is not based upon a consuming desire to "save the lost souls" of mankind. It is the calling, the awakening of an adept, not the adept calling himself. It is the calling of he who has been given the wisdom and the charity through thoughtful reasoning and not the teachings from a denominational seminary that teaches only their dogma. There is such a difference between knowledge and wisdom, and many mistake the former to also be the latter. Therein lies the difference and the greatest of dangers, leading the people farther into the desert as Moses and the priesthood led the Israelites. It was Joshua (synonym for "Jesus") who led them across the river Jordan to the promised land.

We must recognize this difference. The world is filled with knowledgeable people, many of which are egotistically brilliant. But a very small minority is full of wisdom and charity. Some of the greatest criminals have been very well educated and knowledgeable, but lacking the wisdom needed to lead the proper way of life. The world's governments are filled with many very great and knowledgeable minds, but wisdom and charity is rarely found in the world of politics. They must first be led by their political party which is not even a part of Congress or the White House.

Our studies of science has shown us how wrong even popular knowledge can be if not examined in the light of reason and proven fact. Man would never have stepped upon the moon if reason and fact had not prevailed and the law of relativity had not been accepted. We found that light was not instantaneous but had a constant speed of 186,000 miles per second. It was finally a proven fact that the earth was round, that it and the planets circled the sun, and the heavens were filled with unlimited galaxies filled with billions of blazing suns. We have found the universe to be of unimaginable dimension, and everything within it traveling at tremendous speeds. We have also found that the earth, 93 million miles from the sun, circles it in a year's time. Science has not been a curse as the religious world has proclaimed, but rather the opening of knowledge of our beginning and our climb upward, out of the slime pits of creation.

So we find that even with the abundance of great knowledge, there still must be a factual realization of these mystical powers behind all the physical forms that exist. There must be a cause, a need for a formation to be as it is. Who, for instance, formed the first idea of a ruling deity sitting somewhere in a mythical heaven? Upon what facts were these ideas formed? It is time for us to face reality and turn from these myths and gods of ancient assumptions to the laws of the universe.

Wisdom and charity are gained through a hunger and desire for an understanding of the world around us, and an insight of what is true and right and lasting of our knowledge, bringing to our minds the ability of good judgment. Wisdom is the understanding and using of our knowledge for a better way of life - for all. Charity is the love and the oneness of all things that is awakened with this wisdom. Far too often empathy is mistaken for charity, but without love, charity does not exist.

Mass slaughter of millions of innocent victims by the early Roman Catholic Church, by burning, by crucifixion, and by the sword was done under the banner of cleansing religion of heresies. Wisdom and charity has been burned at the stake by the very leaders that were to lead the people to heaven. Millions of books were destroyed through the ignorance of protecting the minds of the people.

The time has definitely come for a spiritual awakening, unveiling the theologies and beliefs that fill our world so that people can understand the true path that Jesus taught, the Kingdom of God within all.

-6-

The Fallacy in Religions

To the surprise of many in the search for truths is the realization that our religions are only the beliefs in and reverence for a supernatural Power that we have been told is the creator and governor of the universe. In the world of psychology that deals with the mental psyche and its illusions, notably brought out by C.G. Jung, it is noted that our thoughts and beliefs are arbitrary illusions of our assumptions and judgment. Ideas exist almost everywhere; we are deluged with them constantly.

From our birth we are indoctrinated into the beliefs and doctrines of our parents, our friends, our government, and even in much of what we read. It is only after we reach an age of reasoning that we can begin to weigh this phenomenon, if we choose, in the light of unfettered knowledge. Where did it all begin? Perhaps this knowledge was given us in Sunday school, where we learned about Adam and how he "fell from grace" by disobeying "God", and how Jesus saved us by his blood sacrifice to the

Father. Perhaps we were also told the story of creation, the story of Noah and the flood, of the baby Moses hidden in the thrushes, of the Red Sea parting, and the Ten Commandments written by the "finger of God".

These were the myths and legends passed down from the ancient writings of Judaism that were the basis of their claim to be The Chosen people. But none of these stories told of the spirit within man, but rather of a divine power in the heavens that presides over the will of the people. It also told of their deity, Jehovah, a jealous and vengeful God who led them into the annihilation of their enemies for the land promised to Abraham and his generations.

We must be aware that there are over a hundred different beliefs, and many with their own names for their deities. Even Christianity is broken into many denominations, each differing in its own dogma. Its roots, however, are deep within the Book of Judaism. With these beliefs have come many differing concepts that we refer to as theology and dogma, the guides in the rituals of worship of this supernatural Power.

Where did all of this begin? Is it important that we strive to understand the beginning and the concept of our Christian religion? Or, should we keep our face turned toward the dark wall of ignorance that the world has been facing for many centuries of time, and be content that our faith will suffice? Each of us must one day make this choice and that day is drawing nigh for a vast number that feels a hunger for truth.

We will need to look far back in time, even as far as the archaic Homo Sapiens to find the real answers. From his very beginnings, after becoming conscious of being conscious, which we term his reputed "Fall", by recognizing the world around him and by knowing "good" and "evil", or the ability to make a choice and a decision, there came a time when the feeling of some intangible force controlled the rhythmic actions of everything, from the movement of the stars to the wind in the trees. It was in a time when mankind had been as the animals since time immemorial, being led by intuition until his developing brain lifted him into a higher consciousness of being able to question. Then he became conscious of his surroundings, even of his helpmate that had been at his side, and he faintly began to reason.

Even yet that dim memory of this guiding power (our intuition) still remains in our psychic mind. The pattern is there for us to examine and use if we will. Our hunches, our dreams all are a part of this inner guiding power of the faded past, still there for us to use but very dormant from lack of use.

The efforts of folklore to explain these mysteries back in those days of yesteryear formed the many beliefs in the spirit gods that arose, the gods of power that seemingly were separate from man. The adulation lifted upward to appease these gods became in time what we now term religion. We call most of these old beliefs "paganism". But is there truly a difference from our religions of today as we lift our hands and voices toward an unknown god from those of yesteryear? Examined carefully, we discover the startling similarities.

We find in every race throughout the world this same belief in divine intervention deep within their old mythologies. It was that this divine power also presided over man and brought him the emotional experiences and an alteration of consciousness, that of being a chosen people of this Intangible Presence that the mind had created. Obeisance began, worshipping this fearsome, jealous unknown deity in an effort to receive His blessing and escape His wrath.

63

Through rituals this feeling of spiritual experience could be brought back at will as we find in the pagan races the world over, through their chants and dances - and in the rituals of the religions of our own world. But upon close examination we find it a selfish experience in a manner of speaking, giving the spiritual blessings and experiences to the believers only while all others were outcasts and "sinners". But in truth the rain falls upon both the godly and the ungodly.

The spirit world of experiences has many levels. It can be reached in many different ways. The savages of Africa has used the rhythmic beating of the tom-tom and their ceremonial dances and dress to incite trances and experiences. The early Indians of the southwest used mescaline, also referred to as peyote, as a stimulant for hallucinations in their ceremonies. We find in the churches of Christianity here in our civilized society that the colorful robes, songfests with hands reaching upward, and ritualistic prayers of adoration to this unknown Power in the heavens to incite the congregation.

We also have people in our own society turning to marijuana for its mind experiences. Still others reach out for stronger drugs such as heroin and cocaine for the same purpose. Really not surprising is the fact that many of the users of these hallucinating drugs are regulars in the church world and in our political world as well. Many of those were also the defiant youths of the Turbulent 60's. Thus we find that the conscious mind takes many avenues for its experiences and pleasures.

But the alteration of our consciousness for our personal spiritual experiences and uplifting is not the manner in which to search for a spiritual life. This is the manner of worship that we also find among the fakirs of India as they strive to find their own Nirvana (peace) for themselves. It should be a search for an understanding of the way we should all live together, daily and hourly for that peace which man has been searching for, and for the revelation of the inner power that dwells in each of us. "You must be born again"; there must be a rebirth of thought and understanding, and of doing.

Almost all of these old beliefs and legends are gone now. These were the tales given by the shamans as the people gathered around the nightly campfires of bygone days. At first the shamans were women, for they were the guiding hand of the family, but as time passed it was taken over by the masculine hunters and warriors.

The people listened intently to these first stories that told of their past in mystic tales and of the Great Ones that helped form their crude societies. They were reminiscences of the ceremonies before the hunt. They were stories of how the animals sacrificed themselves so that the people could survive. They told also of the guiding Spirit that created all things; everything was related in life, each specie dependent upon the species below it for its very existence.

Those stories were a truth to those people; they had faith in them. But somewhere back in time the leaders also became the priesthood. They turned folktales into beliefs of gods who controlled them. It became the accepted answer for the control of the masses as the supernatural Gods were substituted for the true search for knowledge of the how and why of life.

Worshipping these unknown gods became prevalent in all the races throughout the world. Egyptian and Hebrew, Zoroastrianism, Taoism, Buddhism, Druidism, Islamic, Judaism, Christianity, all are beliefs in a certain thought pattern for worshipping a deity and all of them believing that it held the Truth. In a sense they were right, for it was a Light, dim though it was, given to those who accepted it, though designed expressly by the leaders for authoritative control of the masses.

So it is with the religions of today. They are a truth to us, because we have faith in what we have been told as truth. In studying the remnants passed down to us we have formed that which we have for our day. We find Christianity as formed by the medieval Roman Church a mixture of Judaism, Zoroastorism, and Roman Mythology. Out of Judaism came Jehovah. Out of Zoroastorism came the two spirits of Good and Evil, or God and Satan. Out of Roman and Grecian mythology came the rituals that prevail - and the days of our week. These were based upon the concepts of the early leaders and agreed upon by appointed councils to be the theology of belief.

But Truth we find is nebulous so that it can lead every mind in any direction that the mind chooses to follow. What is truth to one may be a parable or legend or even heresy to another, so that no one is wrong in his religion as long as it takes him in the direction of his understanding. But the day will come to each of us when a choice must be made, when the knock on the door of our heart is finally heard and the old ways must be cast aside for the True Path. A change must come in our minds. "Ye must be born again."

But remaining in ignorance of the laws of life is the folly, or perhaps the stumbling block for man. Searching for truth is the true responsibility of all of us and there will always be a reward for this effort. "Seek and ye shall find."

The true Laws of Life are the ultimate goal for any attainment, and they must be understood spiritually as well as literally. It is a Way of Life, not a Way of Worshipping an unknown, anthropomorphic deity.

We perhaps might repeat again that this is the time of revelation; nothing is hid any longer. Politics and graft are being uncovered almost daily. Justice is slowly prevailing. So also is esoteric teachings being brought forth and revealing the weakness in our old beliefs and showing us the esoteric side of man. We are spirit, mind, manifested in a form for creative expression.

It is presumed that without the cloak of Christianity over the world we would not survive. As we study history we find this a gross error and perhaps even the opposite would be true. The inhumanity of Christianity and its Holy Wars has decimated country after country under the banner and shield of the Cross. It has killed millions for believing differently. It denies marriage to unbelievers of its dogma, and to the divorced. It does not recognize women as equal to the male. It is a dynasty of absolute power over the people's lives by Church and State, from the purse to the privacy of the bedroom.

We must also note the utter lack of its acceptance of any scientific facts down through time that differed with its beliefs, and the penalties it pronounced upon those who brought them forth. We need only look back to the days of Copernicus and Galileo as an example as they tried to tell the church world that the earth circled the sun. Even yet in our day it is still believed that the earth is only 6000 years old. Such as this cancels the claim of infallibility and being God's only mediator between "Him" and mankind.

There has always been the dream of a perfect world. But, as individual desires blotted out the vision of it being a realistic dream, it became the myth of Heaven to be attained as a reward in the after-life. Long ago Man asked the question, "Am I my brother's keeper?" We have practiced the negative answer for many centuries and it has failed. How easily brotherly love and charity has been cast aside by the cry of irresponsibility!

But now, as calamities wreak havoc upon different parts of our planet, the heart of man is opening and he does become his "Brother's Keeper" to those in need. Empathy is brought out and no effort is too great to relieve the pain and loss of those suffering victims. Suddenly, color and religion looses the old boundaries as true compassion comes forth. Man becomes as a saint in that hour of need, completely separate from Church ideology. He will reach out and offer his own life to save another.

"What greater love hath man that he will give his own life for another." What great tenderness is felt in those words! That is the True man coming forth that we try to keep hidden deep within us almost shamefully. But, in that time of need it blossoms forth and reaches out to the earth and all its creatures.

This is the godliness within man. It shines forth in an overwhelming wave of spiritual bonding. This is not because of religious belief. It is because it is the inner man coming forth, unsung and unmolested. This is the bonding of the spirit within me bonding with the spirit within you. It needs no affiliation with church. It needs no theology or dogma. It is what Jesus taught coming forth from the heart.

The folly of religion down through these many centuries is that it has formed the path of life by the mind-set in what is FELT to be important for control. The Church has substituted feeling and experiences for teaching.

This has been formed by our Nature mind in following the desires of our body senses instead of our intuition of what is truly the Way that Jesus taught.

The Way of Life as portrayed by Guatama the Buddha and Jesus is not the accepted life of today, regardless of the great cathedrals and Houses of God we have erected. Our will has been deluded by the individualistic world in which we see ourselves, the world of vanity and personal attainment. We do not feel a part of the ocean of Consciousness but rather as individualistic drops of consciousness and each striving to be an ocean of power and position unto itself. But a drop does not an ocean make.

We hear the cry of Materialism as being the problem of today. That is the folly of our teachings. The material world is only the form that Self uses for its manifestation. Without form energy is only latent, worthless. Without materialism life would be unbearable. It has brought ease and comfort to a cold, cruel life for the masses, and it has come from out of the spirit world of thought as a need for mankind. How can we preach the evil of worldliness about electric lights and heating, indoor plumbing, the automobile and the airplane, and the thousands of comforts we take for granted in a normal life? These have been a blessing in our world, but far too many still cannot partake because of the individualistic manner of distribution in our society.

Our problem is a mind and will problem, not a material problem. We have not placed Life in its true concept of the oneness of form and the formation of a society for all. We praise our God - and forget all His other children.

The material world is inorganic, not evil. It is our mind that allows our senses and desires to dominate our will. It is through the lack of Charity

69

(Love) and Justice for all that the darker side exists. Our bodies are even desecrated by eating and drinking to satisfy our senses. The time has certainly come for a new revelation to show us a new vision of how to live.

We can begin to realize why there are so many different religions, each with its theology to offer the rank and file. We recognize that each is correct in its light, meant for those in that level of understanding that desire only the milk. But we cannot remain in the medieval age forever. The universe has been opened to us, a grandeur of unbelievable dimensions. Time reaches back billions of years toward the beginning. "God" is the inner spirit of life and love within us, the Consciousness that fills the universe.

A new dawn is breaking over the horizon.

-7-

The Ages of Time

For centuries prophets and astrologers have talked of a coming Age filled with love and harmony that has become the age-old longing deep within the heart of man since his first awakening. Even in our time this vision has been reborn as writers and directors have portrayed this Age of Aquarius in song and dance on the greatest of the world stages, that of Broadway.

The date of its beginning was never exactly prophesied. But we know that our earth spins its pathway through the constellations of space as it circles the sun to give us our seasons. We have also been told that our sun swings in reverse order through these same heavenly bodies as it circles the center of the Milky Way galaxy. This gives us these different zodiacal ages. Thus we have the varying waves of energy to form the different ages, and to form the many different life forms of expression on this planet Earth.

This, then, brings to light the saying, "There is a time for all things." It is the measurement of changes in waves of energy that bombard our planet and the effects and causes of the different ages. These are spoken of in many different ways. Ours is not a closed system as claimed, for we are constantly bombarded with waves of energy coming from far beyond the edge of our space.

Normally we think of time in terms of hours and days and years, and now we have been awakened to the passing of centuries and millenniums. But there are other names we have coined to express time of extremely greater lengths which we now feel it is necessary to recognize as science expands our knowledge of the universe and our place in the realm of creation.

We speak of *aeons of time* as we speak in terms of the universe, when suns have formed and died over billions of years, radiating their waves of energy outward for their allotted life and then exploding into gaseous clouds and elements of matter to form new, more advanced suns. From out of these nuclear furnaces has come the fusion to form the elements of matter that form the planets, the comets and the asteroids, first the gases and then the elements in their allotted time.

The geological time of the earth is measured in *eras* of formation; Paleozoic, Mesozoic, and Cenozoic eras, each millions of years in duration. These are divided into shorter "periods" of time; Cambrian, Silurian, Permian, Jurassic, Cretaceous, tertiary, Quaternary, and Recent, to show the detailed steps in the formation of the earth's mountain ranges and the ice ages, and also revealing the species that have come - and gone - in their appointed time, from the microbe to the dinosaur - and man.

We realize of course that there is the Creationist's belief that denies these eras and hold fast to the literal, spontaneous creation of all things as the bible stories relate it, but that is not for us to question here. We speak only of the signs and the tell-tale evidence that has been found in the earth to proclaim that which once was but no longer is. We are reading the signs in the earth itself, and not striving to interpret age-old writings into a belief.

We also have the earthly *ages* to measure historical events such as the Nomadic age, the Bronze Age, the Iron Age, the Age of Christianity, the Age of the Renaissance, and the Industrial age of our present time. These are the ages recognizing the advances that man has made as his mind and his imagination developed and he began a more positive role in his progress. Slowly he became somewhat of a master over his environment and has shaped it as he deemed necessary.

Then, of course, we have "*The Clock of Destiny*". This is time expressing the movement of our sun and the earth through the twelve constellations of the zodiac in the heavens commonly referred to as astrological signs. Just as the Bible states as we have earlier quoted, that there is a time for all things, so are they recorded in the age designated by the sign in which our sun is traversing at that time; the age of Taurus, Aries, Pisces, Aquarius, etc, approximately every 2150 years through each of the twelve signs, but in reverse direction of the earth's path. We find these ages as moments in history when changes in vibratory waves came to form new and higher concepts of thought for the different races throughout the world.

Thus is our history recorded in many different ways, and we find that "time" is in fact only the measurement of the steps in our evolution or growth. We realize that this measurement of time by the Clock of Destiny is also not an accepted fact by many though we find in the bible the allegorical references to them in The 12 tribes or children of Israel. These consisted of eleven male and one female, with a set of twins as the zodiac itself is named. These signs also record the appointed days of the religious feasts.

Apostle Paul stated that allegories abound throughout the Old Testament to teach us lessons in story form even as Jesus did with His parables. Thus, the creative story of Genesis, the flood of Noah, The tower of Babel, the story of Abraham and the confusing and dispersing of the races throughout the world be only allegories to show how our earth was formed and the many drastic changes that has transpired down through the ages of time.

Let's examine these for a moment so that we may have a better understanding of our ancient past. For it is the study of the past that reveals our progress and failures so that we can visualize the future that we desire to build.

We realize that Creationism believes that the earth was created about 4004 B.C., approximately 6000 years ago, based upon the chronology as given in the bible. This is the basic foundation of Christianity. But this was actually about the time that the pyramids of Egypt were being built, when already a few million people were scattered throughout the earth. Over 600,000 people, without counting the women and children, "followed Moses out of Egypt" as the bible tells us. So we must rely on the facts that we find leading us to a far more distant creation than believed. It is the INTERPRETATION of the biblical writings that has created the problem of time.

The first pages of recorded history opens about 3000 B.C. with ancient Egypt, China, and Babylon already being the seats of early civilization. This was in the sign of Taurus, the Bull, the symbol of strength through material possessions and the beginning of the priesthood. We are learning much about this time in our past from the archeological diggings in this last century to open the pages of history to a broader understanding.

We have also found ancient stone statues and pyramids in other lands showing that the mind is universal in its symbols and rituals in the formation of the different religions throughout the world without being linked in any manner. We have ancient writings that tell of the islands of Atlantis sinking beneath the Atlantic Ocean and the fleeing of the survivors eastward into Europe and Africa. Could this have been the flood of Noah? The topography of the ocean floor attests that it could have been a true legend, though much more proof is needed before it can become a fact.

This age of Taurus lasted until the tumultuous years of devastation in Egypt as spoken of in the bible, possible by comet action that has happened previously to our earth. It was also about the time when the Israelites began their search for their Promised Land. The age of Aries, the sign of the Lamb, was on the horizon as a new era for mankind approached. It opened the Aryan epoch, the age of the prophets as they heard "a voice from out of the heavens" to guide the people, though it took until the time of Jesus to reveal that it was in truth "The voice of the Father within" speaking.

It was the time appointed for the development of morality in mankind. It was to be learned both individually and socially through the effect of suffering for disobedience. To the Hebrews it was the Law of Jehovah as supposedly understood and written by Moses, their prophet for that new era, in order to bring them to a higher consciousness and a controlled way of life. But the Law of Jehovah was actually a law of the priesthood, of harsh punishment for disobedience without feeling and mercy, a law unto death for the transgressor in many cases.

We find that as the Age of Aries began fading about 500 B.C., another new era was opening with India being the seat of the esoteric teachings through Buddha, and the exoteric teachings and advancement of knowledge by the great minds of Greece. The Israelites had all but vanished as a power, with only a remnant remaining and it under Roman rule. The esoteric teachings once again returned to the mystery schools of Egypt with the travels of mystics and scribes throughout the Middle East. Alexandria became the meeting-place of these great minds of that time and the location of a great library. It was here that it is presumed that Jesus studied during his sojourn in that country.

The Age of Pisces was dawning. It was the sign of the Fish in the minds of most people, a symbol that has little meaning in its self. In reality, however, it represented the intersection of two overlapping circles believed in ancient lore to be the symbols of the Age of Reasoning and Enlightenment that would come together in its time. Now it was ushering in that glorious age of the Grecian philosophy and scientific studies and brought man to the great realization of himself as an individual and the power of his mind. Immortal words abounded, especially those of Socrates and Plato and Aristotle; "Know thyself". Analytical reasoning and scientific thinking was born. With this ability to reason mankind was raised to a new level of learning.

But the beauty of form became a religion to the Grecian masses. The athletes of the Olympics became as gods, worshipped in that day much as we do in this modern age. In time it became their downfall.

Soon the esoteric Christ Spirit was revealed as being within mankind, to be sought as our guide as portrayed in the life and teachings of Jesus of Nazareth and His follower, Apostle Paul. It was taught that man was spirit incarnate, though ruled in error by his senses and emotions and not by his will as it was designed to be. He must be "born again" into a higher way of life, by being led by the spirit, the Father within", with love for all of creation.

Thus was the "New Commandment" given the world by Jesus as he fed them "loaves and fishes", the teaching of a new Reasoning and Enlightenment for this new era. Sadly, it was misunderstood by the new leaders of the people after the death of the Great Teacher. They are still looking for the Messiah to restore the kingdom.

Learning, however, will always bring us a great amount of suffering before it will be attained. It can be mental anguish as well as physical pain as we rebel against it. In the life of Jesus we find, "that he learned obedience through the things that he suffered." (Hebrews 5:8). This shows us that he was also human just as we, and he, too, suffered to learn the True Way of Life that he later lovingly taught. We read of his temptations "in the wilderness" and we fail to recognize that this was a man that fought his carnal desires and temptations as all of us truly must. Truly, he chose to give his life for us in the life that he led, that he might show us The Way.

There must comes that time, however, when we must decide to give up our old ways and ideas that are dear to our hearts as we feel the tug of our conscience for the necessary changes that it requires for advancement. The suffering can be negligible if we realize this need and accept it eagerly as our duty to grow, just as Jesus overcome the devilish, carnal mind within him. This is the renewing of our minds for the reward it can bring to us,

Raymond Moyer

from the passive yin to the active yang of the Chinese and from the negative to positive of the early western world.

We refer to the mind now as being in two parts, the objective and the *subjective.* It can fulfill our material desires as well as spiritual desires, for the material no longer is the whole world to us but only the necessities of life. This is the New Birth as spoken of for this new age.

If we do not heed this voice of our conscience, the Father within, suffering comes in its many degrees of effects. It is not as a punishment, however, as has been so wrongly taught, but rather it is only the effects from the causes of our own doing. If we play with fire we will be burned. If we hate, someone will be hurt, even ourselves. If we love, others also are lifted up.

The wrong-doing under the Law of Jehovah required its certain punishment for every act. But the blood sacrifice of the innocent animal to cover the sins of the people was substituted by the priesthood of Aaron in an effort to bring them to a life of higher morality without the necessary suffering. This is brought forth so vividly in Isaiah 1:11-20. It has never been recognized that Jesus taught that the Law was fulfilled in the new Commandment of Love, for it brought a "sacrifice" of the old way of life for a new birth and life to the person.

These sacrifices of the "Old Law" were contrary to the immutable Law of Cause and effect, for, though the Priests forgave the people through rituals and the blood sacrifice of an innocent animal, there was no balance derived, no "effect" on the person for the "cause" he had done, It brought no end to their tribulations. In its failure it left the people free to continue transgressing without the realization that their suffering would end only with the necessary changes in life that must be made. But this practice

78

continued on into the early Roman Church, even so far as charging a fee for the priest's forgiveness, comparable to the transgression. This became one of the basic reasons for Martin Luther to condemn the Church and break away.

The Law of Moses was a law unto death, with no reward for a life of fulfillment. Its fulfillment was only the coming of a Messiah to rebuild their beloved Israel to its original glory. This was the only fulfillment of the promise as understood in the story of Abraham.

Surely we can look back over these last 2500 years and find that this age of Pisces was the awakening to the need for a new realization of one's responsibilities. It was not for all to accept at that time, but only a nucleolus such as Apostle Paul and his close followers, to continue the teachings of Jesus until the time would come for all. It was more a time of the preparation of adepts for the next era to teach the people of the Kingdom of God within each. The masses still needed to be led by symbolic rituals and dogma until their eyes could be opened to the New Commandment, "that we love one another".

The new age of enlightenment began to appear with the Renaissance and the philosophers that came forth after Martin Luther broke from the Church.

By the 19th century there came the realization of a new theosophy in the teachings of Helena Blavinsky from out of the ancient Hindu writings. Also the studies and writing of Charles Darwin began to appear to shake the religious world.

There have been many "systems" devised down through these times to lead man toward a higher plane of living. Each system or belief has had its own name for its deity according to its race. Few, however, have taught of a consecration of the will of the person to follow a new Path, a true At-one-ment with the inner spirit. They have offered instead a feeling of spiritual ecstasy through faith in their teachings and rituals that proclaim only glorification to the offered deity. But without a rebirth, a change of heart and consecration of our mind and will on factual entities, there can be no reward of this higher plane of living, for we must live it rather than only believe it.

We find that another age is beginning to open before us, the Age of Aquarius. The vision of a new era is truly beginning to unfold. Old ideas are being rejected and new theories are taking their place. No longer is the earth the center of the universe as Aristotle taught and the Roman Church still accepts as fact. Man is now being recognized as only another life-form on a tiny planet in an arm of one of billions of galaxies. Perhaps other planets in our own galaxy have their life-forms also, and possibly even similar to ours. But man's duty here on this planet, if duty exists, is to become more Godlike; loving and creative, knowing the difference between Good and Evil.

So, we find that it is our beliefs that are now being tested in this new age. The vision of a new concept of life is beginning to stir in the minds of many. It is reminiscent of the days of the Renaissance of the 14th and 15th centuries as a new era of enlightenment and reasoning crept out of the dark ages of the Church and State Inquisition as science and philosophy began to flourish. Great minds once again felt free to come forth with new ideas. It brought also the rebirth of old, forgotten teachings that had long been buried by the authoritarian Church rule.

Almost as a duplication of the Grecian Age of Reasoning that opened upon the world about 500 B.C., mankind was once again striving for a new way of expression. This New Age blossomed at a time of great prosecution, both by the Spanish government and the Roman Church to stop the Protestant and other "heretical" movements that had arisen. It was the great uplifting for mankind, with literature, philosophy, and the arts coming forth to free the mind of the Church and State.

Martin Luther had cast the bonds of the Mother Church aside and the fears of its suppression were fading. New thoughts abounded. Beautiful music filled the air with Bach and Mozart and other great musical geniuses. Delicate hands formed works of art out of stone and with brush that are still treasured to this day. The Western World was awakening to a strange new, invigorating feeling, the feeling and longing for freedom, both of mind and body.

The 17th and 18th centuries that followed brought the view of Deism in England, the thought that a certain amount and kind of religious knowledge is inherent in each person or accessible to all through reasoning. They denied the validity of the teachings of any church or any claims based on individual revelation given only to the leaders, for they felt the spirit is universal.

With it came the doctrine of Empiricism, that all knowledge is based upon experience. This was brought forth from the minds of two philosophers named John Locke and Francis Bacon. Opposing this thought came another called Rationalism, with followers such as Descartes, Spinoza, Hume, and Mills. They perceived that through reasoning the mind could formulate a knowledge of truth.

Many of the philosophers of these times believed as Plato had surmised in 500 B.C., that the highest moral and ethical good is basically the same for every individual. Out of this thought came a branch that maintained that the highest good for each individual is what each finds for themselves. This was the belief of a Danish philosopher named Kierkegaard about 1850. He called it Existentialism. It was the belief that the fundamental problems in each individual's life defy a systematic philosophy that has a logical, universal standard which all must meet, under the authoritative rule of Church Council. He believed that there must be the freedom to reason and choose through one's personal experiences to arrive at one's own moral standards and truths.

One's light (understanding) is not the same as another's, and in fairness he cannot be held to a higher realm than his own understanding. "His faith was accounted for righteousness" as we find in the allegory of Abraham was the foundation of this belief, with the thought also that we are all different. It was the lack of the ability to be accountable that brought the medical profession to the study of Psychology, the study of the mind and its differences, and the ability to council and correct any deficiencies that would inhibit better understanding.

We can readily see that philosophy was beginning to weigh many differing thoughts, searching for the nebulous Truth. The power of reasoning was coming forth. It was the consensus of the religious world at that time, however, that a committed Christian life must follow the ideals and rules as set by the church body.

This brought another Existentialist named Nietzche to maintain opposition to this type of moral conformity for it reduced life to a controlled sense of existence by committee instead of the personal responsibility of the individual for the life committed to. He believed in an inner self, an "Overman", to guide the mind to manifest its own manner of creativity and its own individuality. Psychology has recognized this inner self and has called it the psyche and the Id.

Herein was the motivation for the vision and imagination for true growth within each individual. In essence it repeated the teaching of Jesus, "The Father in me, He doeth the work." But again the condemnation of the church was overpowering and the zealots of religion again buried the new ideas, just as the later teachings of Darwin were ridiculed and buried by later religious zealots in our country. The Church once more maintained its authoritative power over the people.

With these new metaphysical thoughts, however, came the freedom of the materialistic desires that had been latent in man for so long. It brought a transformation to the world of a new society, a renaissance that marked the transition from the medieval age to the age of artistic thinking as man began to create in form that which he imagined in his mind. The age of invention and industrialization was on the horizon ready to take its turn in the growth of society for a better way of life.

Being religious minded people, however, the majority still does not believe in the evolving of thought and knowledge as brought forth in these ages as spoken of. Even yet it is dismissed as paganism and heresy. They scoff at the revelations of science; they do recognize, however, the effects of the sun's rays upon us, the moon's effect upon the tides and our emotions, and the bible story of the three pagan Magi who saw in the heavens the sign of the coming king of Israel who, we are told, was the baby Jesus. But denominational beliefs still reign supreme and dismisses that which does not agree with their dogma.

We have continued on in our materialistic ways with faith that God will intercede and answer our call for help without the true renewing of

83

our minds and the searching for ways to build a better society. But so far our cries have been in vain as the desires of the carnal mind has continued to rule over the spiritual world and we have continued downward.

It is not a question, then, of whether we believe in these ages or not. We can already see the many signs that man is turning to a more softer, helpful way than has ever existed. The United Nations has been formed in an effort to bind countries together more peacefully and to help the stricken ones. The Red Cross and the many other similar organizations rush to the aid when calamities happen. Welfare to the needy and Social Security to the aged are efforts of humanitarian help never before known. We can envision that the Age of Brotherly Love is not far around the corner - if we will strive a trifle harder.

So many individual efforts have been made to help in times of need that makes us realize that we are, indeed, conscious of a greater empathy that ever before. The list could go on as even more changes come. We find that the male-dominated church world is beginning to crumble with the female compassion coming forth throughout these different channels, though the female is still denied equal status and barred from the pulpit by the male ego.

But scientific research is slowly replacing religious belief based on faith alone. No longer are we the center of God's domain as we have been taught by theology for so long. The throne of our anthropomorphic god is disappearing from just above us as our space probes search the heavens. We have become only lonely infinitesimal dwellers on a rather small planet in the Milky Way galaxy. It in turn is only one of billions of other galaxies each formed with their billions of suns such as ours, in a universe reaching trillions of light years in every direction. We have shrunk to only a speck on a minute planet in a universe so vast that comprehension is an utter impossibility.

But even science is based upon the materialistic answer to all problems, with esoteric thought left to the literal-minded churches, a sad day for humanity. We cannot continue to base our beliefs on faith alone as dictated by the exoteric councils of men that are in control while our earth slowly dies. We must open the door to the inner mind and the possibilities that exist.

So far our knowledge and efforts in this past twentieth century have greatly surpassed the glorious days of Rome and the Grecian empire, even the grandeur of the Renaissance. Studies such as anthropology, psychology, geology, cosmology and ontology have come forth, searching for a better understanding of the miraculous creation of which we are. The scientific world has come forth with advances in the fields of medical, transportation, and industrialization never before dreamed possible, far outstripping other centuries though the groundwork had previously been made by earlier minds. Now the high-tech age of the crystal chip has opened another new age of miracles and wonders far beyond what ever could have been imagined.

There should be no question that another new age is truly beginning to unfold. Old ideas are being rejected and new theories are taking their place. The myths and legends of ancient yesterdays which had been so literally accepted for these many centuries are now being understood in a new, mystic light. The realization is coming forth that religion, just as science or any study, must be founded upon proven facts and not accepted entirely by faith alone, and change must come as our knowledge increases.

For the inner mind of man is striving to come forth and lead us to a better way.

"Come, let us reason together." This must be the ruling thought in our lives as we strive to bring balance to our suffering world. It is our duty - our responsibility actually - that each of us rule our lives both morally and spiritually, with the Law written within each heart instead of only on pages in countless law books as it has been for so long.

Only then will we be able to see that Golden Era become a reality. Only then shall we be able to see God - in every face and form around us.

-8-

The Immutable Laws of Life

Sometimes, in the writings of the great mystical minds that have flowed down through the ages there comes a line, or a phrase perhaps, that is indelibly marked to be an unforgettable quotation. "I Am". "Know thyself". "Weigh all things; keep that which is true". "There is nothing to fear but fear itself". "To be or not to be". "I have a dream". The list is almost endless.

Each of us no doubt has such a phrase always in the back of our mind, ready to come forth in time of need. These will usually lift our minds to a higher plane of thought and a moment of contemplation on a deeper truth and perhaps even a better way of life. It can also act as a reminder of the Path we choose to follow.

Such a one is found in the sonnet of "As You Like It", by William Shakespeare, truly one of the great minds of the western world.

"All the world's a stage and all men and women merely players, each with his own part. They have their exits and their entrances, and one man in his time plays many parts, his acts being seven ages."

In writing these words Shakespeare left many thoughts and questions unanswered. Who was the playwright of this great worldly masterpiece that he hinted of? Who were the appointed choreographer and director? Was there a divine plan written from the beginning of time as hinted, and are we the players, acting out our part as, upon cue, we enter the stage of life?

Just how are the parts assigned? Were we, as tiny infants, tossed upon this great stage of life under the tutelage of our untrained parents and our environment through our formative years, then later expected to direct ourselves through this great Drama of Life in a certain prescribed manner?

Or, could it be imagined that there were really no assigned parts and lines, but only an empty stage called Earth had been created and each of us must accept a part and position as handed us, lowly though some might seem while others so very high? Thus will we be judged for our performance after our short curtain call. Or will there be many "practice" curtain calls until each part is an act of perfection? This would be reincarnation into other lifetimes

Perhaps the most common consensus is that we think of ourselves as having a free will to think and to do as we so desire. Our code of ethics is as we choose it to be. We are expected, of course, to stay within the guidelines of the Justice and moral codes of society. At times some are commended by their peers for a performance well done - in the eyes of the beholders. Many times even the codes are stretched to their very limits as our desires reach for the gold ring of success without regard of other actors on the stage with us.

But this freedom of choice that we speak of does not in all instances lead to the desired goal of God-likeness, as the part was no doubt intended. Nor does it build a healthy society as we inwardly feel that it should. There is little forethought of the consequences that our actions might have upon others as we are led by our will and desires to do and to possess for our own benefits. Instead, it leads us to individualistic thoughts and desires, which in turn brings forth the carnal life of power and greed, the very conditions we find the world is now drowning in.

We must always keep in mind that it is our inalienable right to adopt the religious beliefs of our choice. Sadly, however, here in the western world until this day there has not been a true choice of religion and belief. It is usually passed from generation to generation. It is rather only a denominational choice of Christianity. With all of the great philosophical thoughts that came forth out of the Grecian era and out of the last 500 years from philosophical minds, none has reached the pulpit for the edification of the masses. They have been buried by religious prejudice.

If the worldly drama had been written for each of us and we acted out our part as written, it would then be a planned performance even as Shakespeare's own masterpieces were written, the end known at the very beginning. This is the belief in an omniscient deity. This is what has actually been taught and believed by the Christian church, that the Son was planned from the foundation of the world (Revelation 13:8). It was therefore known from the beginning of creation that man would fall. He had no choice. Neither have we a choice of birthright.

There are many quotations in the bible that could easily be interpreted in this manner. One need only read Romans 8:28-30 and Ephesians 1:5 and 11. Many have clung to these words and other phrases to form their own beliefs. This is, of course, one of many theories taken from the self-same bible that is used by the many beliefs and denominations of religion, showing that the mind can formulate that which it desires to believe.

It also predicts the literal end times and the rising of the Beast, the Anti-Christ, from out of the sea to give the people his mark. It is a planned future happening that must take place to punish the ungodly, those who were not called to be the chosen. It was feared by many that our social security number could well be the mark. It also has the literal prediction of the saints literally resurrecting their old bodies and being lifted into the skies and flying away into the heavens at a predetermined time.

W find this thought does away with the free-will of man and makes of him only a pawn, giving each an excuse for conduct most unbecoming a human being without there being any personal responsibility of actions. Each of us would be acting out our part as it was written and the ending would be as the script ordained. Therefore, it could be said of our actions, "God made me do it". We would feel no true responsibility in this type of life save the fulfilling of our part as it was written and assigned.

Is not this the way our society is seemingly going? Our responsibility is placed entirely upon the Sacrifice for a crime another had seemingly committed in order for us to think in this manner. We must attribute the human qualities of speech, of hearing, thinking, feeling, and reasoning to our deity. We must make Him a BEING. He is also our accuser. We can look back at the gods of Greece and Rome and find these same attributes assigned to their gods, giving the people nothing more than an anthropomorphic BEING as a deity. Such has the Christian world done in giving these same sensual qualities to its "God", creating a god of form with human attributes and human actions, seated upon a throne high in the heavens.

We, then, cannot think of the universe as being a planned creation and still have our free will. Creation has been an evolving process in the eyes of scientific studies. Evolution has not been a PLANNED growth. It has happened because each step has been a reaction in some manner to a necessity for the Life force. It requires a physical form, an electron, a proton, then an atom and a molecule, forming finally into a complex body. Without this necessity and struggle for manifestation there would have been no formation of all the different species and forms we see all around us, from the microbe to the elephant and on upward to mankind. The Immutable Laws of the universe govern; the law of cohesion, adhesion, repulsion, and gravity creates; the law of entropy destroys as each form reaches its limit of use.

To believe it as a planned circumstance one immediately has termed it as being predestined, the outcome known from the very beginning and we are only actors playing out our assigned parts. Where, then, is our free will, or even the law of Chance?

We find that Christianity as proclaimed by the church-world has many weaknesses. It has given man a spirit BEING as a deity, made of a SUBSTANCE as proclaimed by the medieval Roman Church in the Nicene Creed of 352 A.D. It requires the acceptance of the teaching of a supernatural creation and Adam's sin, and the curse put upon his offspring, also proclaimed by the Roman Church. It sentences us as sinners at birth, criminals in the eyes of our God with our very first breath, with the threat of eternal torment hanging over us if we do not accept by faith the pardon they proclaim He has offered us by the death of His only son.

But everyone is not given the same level of opportunity to receive this message, making it not a gift of grace to all but a gift only to those fortunate enough to hear and believe without question, Is this the manner that we would offer a gift to our children and condemn those that did not accept to a tormented death? I dare say not!

We have found in this last century many facts that have drastically changed this Drama of Life as it was proclaimed. We have discovered that within each atom in the universe there is the spark of the great Universal Consciousness in the form of positive and negative charges of energy. From these simplest of forms from the beginning of time there has been a continual evolving through nuclear fusion and cohesion to more complex forms called molecules. There was no planned pattern, no outline upon which to build, and no past experiences to lean upon. There was only the energy becoming awakened by motion, and the archetype or possibility of every form imaginable that could ever be brought forth was within. Just as the clay and the marble have within themselves the archetype of any figurine we desire to make and yet no pattern or plan is absolutely dictated.

First it was the fusion of gases, then the atoms and molecules for the forms that could support Consciousness or life. Then came the creative ability, the attraction, cohesion, repulsion, and even mutations within itself to further the creation to a higher, more "perfect" form.

Later, as the Homo sapiens arrived on the horizon with a developing brain, the script and the acting were allocated to them. An inner guide was given him which we have named Intuition. His will to do it his way came forth as he strived to learn a better way of expression in the cold, cruel world in which he found himself. As changes in design became a necessity through eons of time each was brought forth in the models that followed. Model after model had to be created for each step upward, and each had to be discarded as a new necessity arose.

We are beginning to understand this a trifle better now as new revelations are brought forth both through science and through the studying of the great esoterical writings of the past. This new awakening is the sudden realization that our lives should have some semblance of meaning, some value far more important than the vanity of our individual struggles that has hindered the attainment of a more perfect society for all. We now can have a new incentive to follow the outline as given us and to act our part as the "director" within shows how it should be performed. A new vision has been offered us and a new way of the why and the how it can be attained.

Just as there are those immutable laws of gravity, cohesion, and even the turning of our earth, so is there a law of life that must be balanced to bring harmony. It is called the Law of cause and effect, or the Law of Karma. It will be spoken of later.

The Laws of the universe have never been taught. We know of the law of gravity. What goes up must come down. The law of attraction and repulsion is plainly seen in the magnetic world as well as the world of atoms. We know it individually by the "interest" felt between man and woman, and the repulsion sometimes felt. We have also heard of the law of cohesion and revulsion. But the law of cause and effect has never been recognized as a law of the universe. It has never been taught. We have been given instead, a promise of "Pie in the sky", a way out of the responsibility of living within the moral laws that man inwardly is conscious of. We must only have faith in a dogma to be "saved".

Can the law of gravity be nullified by faith after jumping from a plane? Can the earth float freely through the heavens without circling round and round the sun? The laws of the universe are immutable, non-cancelable.

Our faith must be in a Truth. Faith, by itself, makes nothing true. It is not an immutable Law. It is a wish.

There is no salvation without works. Something must be done, and done according to the ruling laws. For every cause there will be an effect to conclude it. For every effect there must be a cause for it to happen. This is the immutable Law.

"Whatsoever a man soweth, that shall he also reap."

We have lived in a religious world of Condemnation. But where is our Accuser? "He" has been planted in the heavens by the very leaders who offer us their solution of salvation by faith. The great error that had crept into religion by the early Roman Church leaders was the concept of creation as being a work of perfection from the beginning instead of laws of formation and growth.

This above all shows that mankind has never realized the part that was expected of him to play. He has been ad-libbing his way through life, acting the part of the fool instead of the winning hero. He has never realized that each thought, each action was also a part of the recorded performance that was being judged. Instead, he has been assured that all has been forgiven, or can be forgiven through faith and prayer and penance whenever he decided to make amends. The responsibility of every action has not been a reality to us and we have ignorantly depended upon the slow working of evolution to lift us to that higher plane we know inwardly we should have striven for.

Mankind has needed a higher vision. He has needed the guidance and the script for the scene of Life as it should be played. Jesus and Guatama The Buddha gave the world an outline for our lives to be lived; "seek the kingdom of God within," and "to love one another." The lives of these two great avatars were so similar; the teachings of Jesus were surprisingly a duplication of the latter that was given earlier to another race. Sadly, their beautiful message was deeply buried by church councils and rituals within the first three centuries after Jesus by the Roman government and its appointed Church. Man was then given the theology of Salvation by grace and faith to satisfy him.

-9-

The Law of Change

The one thing that we can be certain of as being permanent in our lives is change. It is undisputedly one of the immutable laws of the universe. Even death is a change, not an ending, for "we" only move from the material body to another realm of which as yet we know very little. But because of this immutable law every moment is different; everything in nature is becoming, never constant.

At the very millisecond of Creation, as "The Spirit of God moved upon the face of the waters", motion and time began, creating change. There is no repeating nor holding onto the fleeting present; in a flash it becomes the past, gone forever, and the future is there before us, waiting. All that exists is the memory, and the thought of what might have been if we had only tried a little harder - and perhaps changed our minds or our actions for a different and better conclusion. The present is all that is in our control, that fleeting moment in time, and it behooves us to use it as wisely as possible, for it is the beginning of our future that lies just ahead.

But changes are very difficult to accept. We desire life to remain constant and serene. We think of our Constitution as written in stone, perfect in every respect. Our Capitalistic system is the ultimate and will last forever. Our religions are indisputable, infallible. But suddenly we are finding that nothing is perfect nor permanent. Change is constantly at work and we must accept it, and the reality that change is a necessity.

But even with this constant change there is still the process of continuity. Man is still man, though he has progressed to a higher level. Animals are still animals, although they, too, have progressed. This continuity is that the original "tree of Life" still remains, but with the differing factors of life through time it has been slowly but constantly changing. More branches and more leaves have been added. Many leaves have fallen, as some forms have become extinct, however, through tragic disasters such as the ice ages that had come - and gone - but they have remained that form until the very last of the specie disappears.

What really changes is the inherent knowledge in each form and its ability to adapt to its environment and circumstances that it faces. This innate ability is present from its originality, not learned or acquired in a just a lifetime.. It has been termed the ability to evolve as circumstances require for continuity.

From the instant of birth our bodies begin the journey through time and change. As the male sperm and the female egg come together, the innate knowledge in the DNA for the building of that form begins its process of formation. Then, in its allotted time it awaits the spirit or soul that will inhabit it and it is "born". From that moment on it follows the path from

98

infancy to adolescence to maturity, to the so-called golden years and then, finally, cessation, or death.

We know nothing of the hereafter; only the story that we have been told of a heavenly home with streets of gold that we will trod upon, dancing and singing our praises to God – if we are "saved". Only then will Change suddenly end and we can rest in eternal peace. This is the dream of fallacy that has been given us and that we have accepted without question.

Man has searched endlessly down through time for the Fountain of Youth in an effort to stop this seemingly senseless pattern of birth and death. Juan Ponce de Leon, in 1512, searched in vain throughout beautiful Florida for this miraculous fountain of Living Water as told in the Indian myths. But the dream eluded him and he died.

So far it has eluded all of those who have searched for a materialistic answer to the esoterically, everlasting, changeless life we dream of. The search, however, still goes on. In the laboratories throughout the world there is the striving to create cells, to cloning, and even embracing the idea of frozen bodies to be awakened in the distant future for a new chance at a new and better life. Man continues to reason that there must be a way to attain eternal life and happiness the easy way. But so far the immutable law of change continues to win and the pattern remains. The Laws of Change and Entropy in the world of form are undeniably immutable.

In the short history of our nation there have been many drastic moments that have brought changes and turning points in our way of life. We have had to adjust. Some of these changes had long and lasting impressions, as the division of our country into the North and South that marked the beginning of the Civil War, and is still a division in the minds of many. The market crash of '29 marked the beginning of the Depression years of the

30's that brought many changes to our nation. So have many other events left their marks; in later years we recognized the effect they brought and the changes that were created.

From the founding of our nation after the great ordeal of the Revolutionary War and the determination to be free that brought victory to a small band of courageous soldiers there came the call to Unity between the colonies and their individual ways of governing. It was no easy task, for each man appointed to form the new Constitution had his own ideas, and his own desires and religion to protect. There were Baptists, Methodists, Quakers and Catholics. There were even Masons, Deists, empiricists and Rosicrucians. There were farmers and there were men of the professions. All had their part in the formation of this great land and government as the ideas and visions of all were coalesced into one unified Constitution of the United States.

It was truly the beginning of American Politics, but what came out of that famous struggle of words and tempers was a work of genius for mankind that stands to this day as a refuge for the oppressed of the world.

One great man, during one of the many tiresome, heated arguments over issues, vigorously stood up and retorted, "Give me liberty or give me death!" Only freedom from tyranny that they had fought so long and so hard for would suffice for Patrick Henry. There was no second choice.

In later years, another great man spoke of it in glowing words that have become a part of our country's history as well. At Gettysburg, President Lincoln stood on the bloodstained hillside overlooking the forlorn battlefield where so many had fallen and delivered his short but solemn message:

"Four score and seven years ago our Fathers brought forth upon this continent a new nation, conceived in liberty and dedicated to the proposition that ALL men were created equal. Now we are engaged in a great Civil War, testing whether this nation or any nation so conceived and so dedicated can long endure. . . . ."

It fell upon a stunned audience that day at the solemn dedication of that blood-soaked battlefield, and President Lincoln felt that he had failed to convey his thoughts and feelings to the nation. The crowd stood quietly as he stepped down from the podium. But as his words sunk deep into the minds of the people gathered there, it was apparent that he had summed it so well in a few memorable words that the speeches that followed were merely bits of flowery phrases. Only history records the name of Senator Edward Everett, the keynote speaker that day, for his name and words never reached that same high level of immortality.

It is well for us to remember Gettysburg where 5,662 men died, 27,203 wounded, and 10,584 captured or missing in three horrible days of slaughter that ruptured our nation ONLY BECAUSE OF DIFFERING BELIEFS AND OPINIONS. The cause of that battle was that the power of reasoning had failed. The effect was the loss and sorrow at Gettysburg.

The War of 1812 called upon us to become a naval power in the world to face the powerful English fleet that tried once again to devastate us. We became unexcelled, even to this day, though many countries have tried. It was a desperate struggle on both land and sea as the new nation of Freedom fought once again the same powerful Tiger of the Seas.

This time a prisoner named Francis Scott Key watched from aboard an English warship a battle so emotionally that he wrote it into a song that has been immortalized. Almost everyone knows these immortal words of America's National Anthem, from citizen to immigrant.

Our nation held fast. We won. It was a triumph to equal the previous war that brought freedom in 1776. One of the great ships of that era, "The Constitution" but more commonly called "Old Ironsides", is still listed as a commissioned ship in our present Navy as a proud reminder of those glorious days of our struggles. Occasionally, she still sails from her home in Boston Harbor to be shown to a new generation, fanning the flames of Remembrance and Patriotism so that we will never forget the struggle to be a free nation.

No history of change in America could be written without the importance of the Louisiana Purchase from France that opened new land to the west. The word "Homestead" was a dream that pushed families to the very limit of endurance as they snaked their way across the prairie-land and across rivers and mountains that should have halted them. But there was no turning back. They pushed on, and they won.

But Not all won the battle of survival; the cost was high in life, agony and tears as the trail was lined with unmarked graves from Independence, Missouri, to the rich lands of Oregon. But out of those hardships came a new breed of Americans, that which we now call The Western Pioneers, a proud heritage for those who followed. The dream in the minds of many pushed the few to accomplishment of the goal. Today the western cities and farmlands are standing memorials to that unquenchable spirit that formed them.

It changed, too, the sedentary lifestyle of the native of the country, the Indians. Their land was invaded and they were pushed back onto devastated reservation lands to eke out a bare existence. Their buffalo, the very heart of their way of life, were mercilessly slaughtered only for their hides, and their carcasses were left strewn across the landscape to rot. Even their beliefs were thrown aside and substituted by the story of a white Savior, while men, women and children were killed and their land stolen and the remainder taken into bondage by the very ones crying to save their souls.

This was a tremendous and heart-breaking turning point in their lives and though there perhaps has been a small healing throughout the years, the scar is still there and occasionally still opened by broken treaties. Though their ways of living was changed from the freedom of range to isolated blocks of worthless reservation land, their minds failed to comprehend the ways of their conquerors.

But the nineteenth century was a remarkable turning point in our nation. The discovery of oil and the invention of the steam and gasoline engines brought forth the Industrial Age. It made power available away from the river and the waterwheel. It brought rest to the animals who plowed the fields and pulled the heavy wagons of merchandise. It also ended the dependence on the wind for ocean travel, for now the ships could carry their own power and set their courses to anywhere on the seven seas whether calm or blustery.

With the steam engine also came the locomotive with a faster and better way of transportation. Soon, twin ribbons of steel began reaching their tentacles from one town to another and the first real people mover and material mover across the land became a reality. In less than half a century it snaked across the continent and opened the West as no other method was able to do. The Pony Express vanished. The covered wagon became only a romantic part of our history, but it left trails of anguish and bloodshed, and graves of loved ones scattered from the banks of the Mississippi to the shores of the Pacific Ocean.

With the twentieth century came the automobile and the assembly-line concept of manufacturing. It brought many changes. It brought drastic changes to our whole way of living, from our home life to our workplace. It stilled the ring of the blacksmith's hammer and substituted with the noise of turning machinery and factory whistles. It erased the stench of the stables and substituted the stench and polluted air of giant chimneys.

Steel mills mushroomed with the influx of this new business. Other businesses also mushroomed into being as satellites of this new industry to fill the needs of the growing wage earnings. People were beckoned off the farms to work in the factories with the promise of weekly paychecks to buy a better, happier way of life.

Many of these new workers were immigrants flocking to our shores to find their pot of gold, but painfully they soon found that Utopia was not just a boat-ride away but only a nebulous dream fashioned in the mind. Instead, they were paid paltry wages and thrust into crowded, dirty tenement dwellings. New skills were needed and education became a necessity for a decent livelihood. The word "Unemployment" was inscribed in our dictionary.

The formation of the Federal Reserve Bank in 1913 was another great turning point for our nation, for it changed our monetary system from government control to Central Banking control. In time, money was no longer printed, but rather notes given to the Federal Reserve Bank for the needs of the Government. It was at that time that we laid the foundation to become a Debtor nation, though it didn't become apparent until our debt became trillions of dollars in the 1980's.

We were heading for another war, this time to end all wars and to bring peace to the world through the League of Nations. But the world was changing as this new nation became the breadbasket and leader as Europe lie devastated.

The Roaring Twenties brought a time of easy money for many and it became a time of speak-easies, bootlegging, gambling, and gangsters, with names such as Pretty Boy Floyd, Bonnie and Clyde, Dillinger - and J. Edgar Hoover to control them. Ammie McPherson and Billy Sunday spread the gospel over the new invention called radio to begin a new era of preaching the Gospel to the lost souls of our nation - and tithing through the mails.

But suddenly the good times ended. In 1929 the stock market crashed. People jumped from the windows of high office buildings rather that face the ruination that soon followed. It was a time of panic never before realized in such a devastating form. Businesses folded. Employment dropped drastically. Breadlines became commonplace in every city. The Great Depression years of the '30's began.

There are many yet alive that remember those devastating years and the drastic changes it brought upon the people. Our nation also became a wasteland of drought, the most severe that had ever come upon our country. The Midwest, from Canada to South Texas, was nothing but a gigantic dust bowl as the rich farmland dried out and became airborne for days on end. The literal story of "The Grapes of Wrath" was being written in the swirling sands and the suffering of the people.

We were fortunate to have a strong president who did what had to be done. He also gave us hope. "There is nothing to fear but fear itself", he encouraged us, and people began helping one another - and being true neighbors.

But as we suffered here in America, Europe was again undergoing drastic changes. Hitler was coming into power and building Germany once again into a great war machine. In 1939 he began by invading neighboring countries with new methods of devastating warfare. Dive-bombers hammered the countryside as panzer divisions of tanks finished the onslaught in a matter of days. No other country was prepared for this new kind of warfare, and though France and England declared war, it was decidedly an unbalanced duel with the Fatherland.

Our way of life changed drastically also. We became the arsenal for the Allies. The price was high in shipping losses. The submarine was one more part of Hitler's plan of European dominance. But our factories began rolling out the needed planes and weapons that brought our nation from its own brink of disaster to a sudden economic burst.

The change in power came as Japan attacked us and we entered the conflict in Europe as well as in the Pacific. Once again the Allies overpowered the Nazi and Italian armies as millions of tons of bombs rained down on the enemy cities and fortifications, reducing them to blazing ruins. Europe was literally destroyed. Hitler committed suicide. His beloved Fatherland died with him.

There is no denying that our nation went through more dramatic changes after World War II. But the moment in time had come. This time changes were beginning in our mind-set, in the way we thought, in the way we understood things with a faint desire to try to do things right for once in our life.

But family life and family values were becoming different as many mothers joined the workforce and children were born to be raised by baby sitters and child-care centers. It became the fad propounded by so-called Help Books written by the New-Thought psychologists to allow even the small children uncontrolled expression and screaming tantrums. "They were only learning to express themselves", we were assured. The "Little Darlings" of the Dr. Spock age took control of their own training, and discipline became only another unused word in Webster's dictionary.

But this was the straw that broke the back of family control. It was the beginning of the fads of long hair and sloppiness, of dope and free-sex living, and the lack of respect for the elders that had always been the dominant cornerstone of our society. Sadly, adolescents no longer visioned a future as generations had in the past, and suicide rates began climbing as young lovers clung together in their own planned deaths. Drop-outs of our schools mounted by the thousands and our welfare system became loaded by single mothers, as delinquent fathers had no feeling of responsibility toward their out-of-wedlock children.

There is no doubt about the transformation brought about by the advent of the Nuclear and Electronic Ages. For a time we alone had The Bomb and the know-how, but that advantage soon disappeared as we found ourselves one day watching a Russian spacecraft circle above us. October 10, 1957 was the day that Sputnik ushered in the true Space Age. A tiny, 184 pound man-made object orbited the earth at 17,000 plus miles an hour, and it could literally be seen as the sun gleamed off its silvery shell as it passed silently overhead.

But our next president, John Kennedy, aimed us for the moon and we jubilantly took up the challenge.

"Ask not what your country can do for you, but rather what you can do for your country," he challenged, and the people of America united once again behind their President as they did on that fateful day in December, 1941, when our Navy was reduced to rubble in those tragic moments of Pearl Harbor.

With our massive array of computers and electronic gadgetry aboard huge shining rockets, we reached that big chunk of cheese first. We stood upon the surface of the moon, in spirit, with the astronauts that braved the dangers for that moment of glory and accomplishment. We, too, took that "one small step for man, but one giant step for mankind" with Neal Armstrong. The material reward for our great effort was an array of rocks as souvenirs and a little something to study in our spare time for signs of life on a barren landscape.

But the dark cloud of division had already crept over us. America had already fought a war we could not win, far away in a country we knew nothing about, and with a bitter ending. It was a high price we paid for a thankless war.. We came back from Korea a defeated nation, and a slowing economy greeted the returning warriors. This time there were no victory parades and no jubilation for them, and the wounds were deep within the souls of all.

We desperately needed a symbol of a winning spirit to pull us together again, and we turned to a military leader in Dwight Eisenhower, for had he not been the political force that bonded the Allies of World War II? He was the Hero loved by all and he could binds our wounds.

But again, from out of a small force of military advisors sent to Vietnam in the late 50's by this great leader grew another conflict that we could not win. It was the breaking point. For the first time in our history patriotic duty was cast aside and rebellion against the Draft and against the war began tearing the nation apart.

Soon the Flower Children blossomed onto our landscape with their guitars and their marijuana, and love in their hearts for all. "Have a nice day" became their farewell wish to all and somehow it seemed the right thing for the whole nation to wish to one other. Old Volkswagen vans were a common sight, painted in various psychedelic colors that became actual homes for many, fitting neatly into their simple, casual fashions and lifestyles.

There were many of those people, however, that made up the Peace Corps and gave their time and a part of their future to help those in need in far away places. They willingly went to wherever there was a need, to teach backward people how to do many things to make life better. They healed the sick. They helped feed the poor. They did what needed to be done with the little that was allocated, with little thanks or enumeration.

Sadly, though, were the many that disappeared from family and friends to lose themselves in Canada rather than face the draft and the war in Vietnam. Right or wrong is not the question now; only that such a sad thing was allowed to happen in our beloved land. Fathers and mothers still grieve over the loss of their "babies" that vanished over the border, so many never to be seen again.

The Age of Materialism was at its peak in bringing changes to our lives. But spiritual thoughts were slowly beginning to enter the minds of many as our ways were being seen as nothing more than vanity, finite and shallow. Most people, however, were still trying to hold to the thought that faith in the dogma of Christianity was the way of salvation.

Has our nation been the only one that has undergone these changes? Sadly, no. The whole history of mankind is nothing more than the record of turmoil as all of the races struggled from early ignorance in their nomadic beginnings to the later building of materialistic societies. Each was first filled with stories of great dramatic struggles for power between the kings, and in these later centuries it has been the struggle for power and the ownership of land by even the masses. For land ownership became a symbol of freedom, and it was the stimulus that settled the new land of America.

This brings us to the startling realization that the great law of the universe is that ALL IS IN CONSTANT CHANGE. There is nothing static. It is either evolving, or it is atrophying. But change is neither good nor bad; it is a Universal Law as is gravity and cohesion. It is what we make of change that makes the difference. It is the mind of man the needs the greatest change.

As we have examined these turning points, and there are countless others of importance and memory that some will remember, we see them as changes in our society and our own private lives, and even yet in so many circumstances we have found ourselves rebelling against it. It is sometimes difficult to understand the need. Some people will adjust quickly, accept it and build upon it; others will die fighting it. Still others will strive for change to fit their concepts by turmoil and tyranny. But it will come, "As night follows day."

And even as it comes bringing these modifications to our physical way of life, to our day-to-day living, so have we seen the great differences come to our spiritual lives. From the ancient days of sacrificing young children, through the dark, horrible days of medieval Europe, through the witch-hunts of Salem, Massachusetts, when believing differently could easily mean death by burning even here in our own religious country, we have seen the spiritual life slowly progressing as new voices are being heard to bring further advancement in knowledge and understanding. We heard a great voice in our time call out, "I have a dream . . .", and his race heard and embraced his words as a new hope for a new freedom. The dream of Martin Luther King is still awaiting true fulfillment, but it brought changes.

Now, as one century closes and a new millennium opens for us, we are beginning to see a new thought and a new wave of enlightenment coming to more and more people. The old ways no longer suffice. A tiny orbiting sphere brought an awareness of space and soon we discovered a universe so vast that it shocked even the scientific world. We saw the workplace of our God spread over billions of LIGHT YEARS, replacing our early concepts of our deity and that our earth being the center of the universe. Now our earth was only a tiny blue speck circling a sun in an arm of the Milky Way galaxy with billions of other suns. We saw the nebulae fashioning a new star before our very eyes and we realized that we were seeing how our own solar system was created.

This realization has brought a different understanding of creation. Suddenly, we realized that the earth really wasn't the center of the universe after all as we had been told for so long, and that, just maybe, man wasn't quite as important in the great universal plan as he had always imagined.

The mysteries and symbols of the ancient writings are being understood in a new light, bringing with it a new awareness of the relationship of man and his God. Jesus had said, very simply, "The kingdom of God is within you." Some are beginning to realize the true meaning behind these simple words and are looking inward for guidance instead of upward for "salvation".

Even as in the days of old, we can now look upward and see the signs in the stars of a new dawning. A change is coming whether we believe it or not. At this moment we haven't the faintest notion what it will bring, but man has a hope within him that it will be that which was prophesied would come, a new world. Bur we will have to build it.

Was not even the coming of the Messiah prophesied to be shown in the heavens as a sign that all could see? We are told that the Magi of Persia saw and understood, and they came seeking the new King of Israel. They found a new-born child, lying in a manger. It was a far cry from the bed of nobility that they had envisioned.

We, too, must find that same Christ-Spirit, not in the nobility of Heaven or the brick and glass sanctuaries which has been created for worshipping our deity - and into which we bring our tithes - We will find it lying quietly in the kingdom of God within our breast.

-10-

The Constant Search

There are many theories that have been brought forth by thoughtful reasoning with a factual and/or an empirical point of view that is not entirely based upon faith and emotional feelings as is theology. This is both the unconscious and the conscious mind at work together, striving to formulate the proper way of life without the rituals and symbolism to conjure only experiences. These also bring an experience to one, but it is the experience of freedom and accomplishment of being guided toward Truth. This comes forth as the promise was given us, "Seek and ye shall find".

Strangely enough, the human mind has failed down through time to recognize the tie between the unknown powers of the universe and ourselves through our intuition or the True Self within. Instead, we have clung to this "God" given to us by our minds, a heavenly anthropomorphic Spirit Being separate from ourselves.

We have always been told that we are weak and alone. The tie we have striven to form with this separate God has been through these rituals of sacrifices, prayers, and glorifications, the very actions we have termed as paganism in the lower races. Any weaknesses we have are only because we have failed to realize the great powers within our inner mind and how to call upon them.

Jesus said, "The Father within me doeth these things, and greater things shall ye do." We find this still true as the stream of inventions and scientific discoveries of this age has flowed from the mind of man. Healing has been accomplished in so many of our deadly diseases, and even the mind has been freed through consultation and meditation. The day of casting out devils has given way to true healing practices through knowledge of medicine and surgery as needed, and physiology as needed for the mind.

We have formed this pattern of worshipping a deity in the heavens that we know absolutely nothing about save through theology's myths and teachings of a supernatural Creator. Now we find that creation really was not a supernatural happening, but rather nothing more than the Law of Cause and Effect in action as the universe collapsed in upon itself with the resultant "Big Bang" to start anew.

These many religions with their countless branches that seemingly worship the same unknown deity with differing dogma has been a very dividing phenomenon, bringing atrocities and wars of unbelievable horror between the differing beliefs and races instead of the Brotherly Love that it was to bring.

This searching for the spiritual must be pointed in the proper direction so that more will be revealed to us as we grow. "Seek and ye shall find".

That is still our admonition. A guide or guru - a minister - can be helpful only in the respect of keeping the focus upon the Path. But one will find only the Path that has been revealed to this guide which has led to many different Paths for different people. There must be the recognition of the personal thought and the revelation to be gleaned for the individual's personal need and growth through deep meditation and reasoning. It is well to be found in the quietness of our own "closet" or the "mountain" that Jesus always climbed for his solitude. But you cannot dream my dream and I cannot dream yours. Each must find the Way to grow in the light and knowledge that each of us possesses, through seeking.

Perhaps an example will show it more plainly. At the time of Martin Luther and his revelations people listened and accepted his teachings, "We are saved by Grace and not by works". It was not a revelation to them in the true sense that it was to Martin Luther but it was a new and easier theological teaching to draw the people out of the Roman Catholic Church.

It was the same instance with Apostle Paul and the great revelation of the Christ-Spirit that came to him. To the people it was only a teaching and it was not a true revelation to them as with Paul. The "milk" of his message was all that many desired and he rarely could give them the "meat" of his message. It worried him enough that he warned them of this weakness in their belief as he tried to lead them upward.

Thus it is that the masses accept only the revelation of a leader and blindly follow him, striving to receive the same spiritual uplift the leader had received through the rituals that he now teaches them. They receive their *spiritual experiences* but never grow in the deeper spiritual concept

115

of the Way through their own revelation. Even the leader is content in his own kingdom of knowledge and refuses to seek any further.

This is what the new spiritual consciousness is revealing to people now. No longer must we be satisfied with a belief in a dogma. No longer must we follow the TV evangelists as they thump their bibles and expound their great Plan of Salvation for the tithes that it brings and for the grandeur it builds. We must seek the guiding spirit within for our daily living. We must seek a new vision, a new way of life. We must seek At-One-Ment with the Christ Spirit within us.

This is the Spirit that comes into our bodies with the first breath and begins striving to build a more perfect temple for itself. But soon the teachings of parents and the care received in its environment begin to interfere with this Builder within, and the will of the child never learns the true way of life. It learns the same carnal, sensual way that mankind has formed since that eventful, mythical day when he "left the Garden of Eden" as his carnal mind began leading him instead of his intuition.

"Without a vision the people perish."

True religion is the Oneness and Unity of all. It is gained by an inner revelation through deep meditation of this great mystery that surrounds life and a great overpowering desire (seeking) for a better understanding. With this wisdom comes the gift of divine love (charity). But without this desire for a deeper revelation we deny changes that must come. Only in such a manner of living and seeking can man reach adeptship and true Oneness with the Supreme Power. That is the way that Guatama the Buddha and Jesus came to their deep revelations.

Each race has had its avatars to teach the people these truths. This is what Jesus, the Buddha of India, and Zoroaster of early Persia taught to their respective races, both nearly word for word though many years and many miles separated them. This, too, is the meaning for the Sanskrit word, Yoga, the union of the self with the Supreme from out of which it came. Is not this the true gospel which Jesus taught?

Another such an adept was the legendary Moses as we look for examples. He was filled with knowledge gained by the years of initiation in the Mystery Schools of Egypt as he grew to manhood. He was taught the secret powers of the heavens and how to control them through astrology. He was also taught the secrets of magic. But through the years he learned empathy for the affliction of his own people as he saw them suffering for existence.

He learned wisdom in the "forty years" he spent in the desert country of Midian and in the household of Jethro, the Priest, who later became his father-in-law. Of what belief was Jethro we have not been told but we can surmise that he was not Hebrew nor Egyptian in this desert country. One might presume that it was of the same order as Melchezidek, another True Priest of the Supreme with only a slight recognition given in the bible and with no affiliation given with race or creed.

It was here in this quiet, peaceful desert country that the understanding of the True God was first revealed to Moses. Here he received his initiation by water. The legend tell of his coming to a well (a source of esoteric truths) wherein "seven maidens (virgins)", signifying purity, were pumping water. He helped them to water their flock. We find nearly this same story in the life of Jesus and also in the story of Rebecca as she was chosen as wife for Isaac.

Then came his initiation by fire on Mt. Horeb (on a mountain top, as was Jesus) as he beheld the bush burning but not being consumed. He saw the "light" of revelation within nature, but there were no "flames" of personal desire to destroy it. In his mind was revealed that there was a creative intelligence within ALL, and in the universe itself, that great and mysterious I AM, or Consciousness.

It could easily be presumed that the teachings of Jethro, the High Priest, of the ancient mysteries was absorbed in a knowledgeable mind that was hungrily opened to wisdom.

It was only after these initiations and the overpowering revelation and wisdom that Moses was able to lead the people of Israel out of the Land of bondage (Egypt). Even yet, he denied he was competent enough for the great task of leading people.

Moses gave his followers the Law to bring forth morality. "Thou shalt not . ." The Priesthood of Aaron gave them a way of sacrifice in payment of wrong-doing instead of the effects that error should have brought. But we must realize that these people were not advanced enough to truly understand the teachings of rebirth, the renewing of the mind, even if it had been given them verbally. This message had to wait many centuries for the coming of Jesus for the true revelation of oneness and "the Father within".

Thus was ushered in what has been termed the Age of Aries, a time of a new way of life for man, the giving up his nature desires for a life of being led by the inner spirit. Instead, the sacrificial blood offering of the innocent animal was substituted by the priesthood for repentance, with no change in the people.

We find the same symbol of revelation in the Book of Acts, chapter 2. We read of the mystical cloven tongues of fire dance among the people, though none were burned as it sat upon each of them. But these people whose leader had been slain now had to choose the path they were to follow. Peter stood up and became the new leader, leading them back into the Judaic teachings of repentance, baptism, and circumcision, rituals instead of changes of thought.

We can begin to grasp, then, that religion is meant to bring us to a change of thought, a new birth, the complete renewal of the mind to a new, loving way of life. It is not just the ritualistic adulation of a Deity separate from us. "Old things pass away; all things become new."

Theology is the teachings that separate us into factions and in turn creates the divisions that has brought forth the holy wars and the genocide, even to this day.

Ministers are trained in the dogma of the church. They dare not reason for themselves for their cloak of power would be stripped from their shoulders. They are only as John the Baptists crying in the wilderness of ignorance, "Prepare ye the way of the Lord!" The true message of the kingdom of God within each which Jesus brought to the world is only now being brought forth once more.

He taught of what is now being revealed by psychology that the psyche within us is the great universal mind that has been striving to lift us to a higher plane of realization and thought. He taught of the God within, not the God far away in Heaven.

We have read in the myths of Genesis countless times no doubt that God talked to Adam as they walked together in the Garden. We are finding in these later days a new revelation of this mystery. God is not a form, a Spirit BEING, that walks with us and talks to us, but is that inner consciousness that awaits recognition so that it can tell us what NOT to do.

God is an essence that becomes a part of us, a spiritual feeling and phenomenon that comes to us through our inner mind. God is Love. God is Mercy. God is Justice. God is beauty. God is Nature. God is the Rose of Sharon. God is the homeless and the hungry we pass on the street.

We are taught that God POSSESSES these essences. But God IS these essences. He is not a FORM that can possess but rather that essence that can be felt as a part of ourselves when we find it.

How sad it is that we have been deceived through these many centuries of the beauty we could have had, but having been satisfied with experiences and not a revelation such as Paul received instead!

We must learn to listen in the silence to hear this guiding Voice. Only then will we find true religion which man has been yearning for down through the ages of time. It is the voice of the psychic mind or the very soul of man striving to guide him. It is the voice ignored by religion as they cry towards the heavens for guidance and blessings. It speaks to us through intuition and hunches, and through dreams, trying to make us aware of even the common psychic disturbances or neuroses we have that cannot be cured by prayer or medical treatment. These must be treated by psychological means which studies both the mind and body. It is even the pages of a book we pick up, or words we hear that opens a door.

So very little is known about the influence of the body over the mind. It has been found, however, that many conclusions regarding the psyche can be inferred from the constitution of the body itself. This brings to mind the age-old study of astrology in order to help understand man, and also the studies of phrenology and palmistry. These have been considered totally unreliable and of pagan ancestry by both science and theology, but much has been proven true regarding the factor that birthplace and birth-date has upon the personality and characteristics of a person.

Mankind is made in many different types; thinkers, dreamers, sensationalists, intuitionalists, introverted, extroverted, rationalists, philosophical, scientific, and even tall, short, medium, dwarfish, fat and slim. Can all these types be fitted into one type of belief in salvation or of an after-life? We think not. We cannot all follow the same drummer, or all dance to the same tune. We are all individuals, each with a brain to fit our body, and each with the gift of reasoning to fit our pattern of life. We should never judge another, but rather analyze our own shortcomings.

The psyche within all of us came from the same source, the great Universal Intelligence. But each of us has been given a different calling according to the gifts we have been given to fulfill it. Each has a different lesson to be learned. We must learn it. It may take us lifetimes, but we WILL learn it through the suffering that our refusal brings.

That is why the awakening is coming now to those who seek a new and better way of life.

We can be assured of one thing; the Prodigal Son does return home as the parable states. The Lost Sheep of Israel WILL be found. It is not the old race of Israelites that became lost and scattered; it is the esoteric children of all nationalities that will return to the real religion of God-likeness, full of wisdom and charity, free at last from the stranglehold of ignorance.

-11-

The Search Continues

We have come now to the time when a new millennium is before us and we can look up with a new awareness to life. The dawn of Aquarius of a new era is on the horizon, lighting the spiritual sky with its beautiful glow and refreshing "water". An age of new hope is dawning to a indifferent world, and the dawn always brings an awareness of a new day. Once again a spiritual enlightenment is beginning to peek over the Mountain of Darkness that has covered us for so many centuries, flooding us with new understanding and a new awakening to the meaning of life.

Just as the age of Pisces that dawned some 2500 years ago brought forth the age of reasoning, inventiveness, and the growth of creativeness with the opening of the mind, so we now find Aquarius bringing forth the spiritual awakening and the revelation of the Christ spirit lying dormant within us, awaiting to be born into reality. Man is discovering who he really is, a Son of God, an offspring of Consciousness.

As we look back through history we see that the past 2500 years has been a time that a greater portion of mankind than ever before developed a desire to learn, to think for themselves, to reason, and to create. But for a time the knowledge gained had been basically of the materialistic part of life and religions had been the substitute for the true path that the prophets, Buddha and Jesus, taught their followers. This pattern, it seems, has had to be for man to evolve enough to realize his great and wonderful potential. The material world has been a blessing in so many ways, but sadly, advantage has been taken by the few over the many, and deep sorrow has prevailed.

In this last century knowledge at all levels has exploded. Now man is beginning to realize that he is a three-fold entity of body, mind and spirit instead of only a living body. He has within himself the innate ability to control somewhat his own destiny, able to help evolve faster by his efforts and spiritual desires than by waiting for the slow, methodical ways of nature that has proceeded in the past. We can see how many have been able to lift their materialistic way of life to a greater level by more education, although, sadly, it is not for everyone. Wisdom must be sought to understand the meaning of life.

But learning can be a slow, tedious, and unexciting process if we allow it. Unless the desire to know is a dominant factor in one's life it is easier to drift through life believing the fashionable and accepting only the inevitable. But the desire to know the things of the spirit can become as consuming as the desires for other knowledge. Then we can realize that there is a time and season for everything, and all things will be revealed in just that way, in its time. With this realization comes an inner peace known in no other way.

Religion, then, should be the teaching of a better way of life for us, not just a way of belief. We recognize that there are many different religions and levels of religious understanding to fill the needs of the many different peoples in the world, and for this we must be thankful. Perhaps it is a beginning to a higher realization. It has been as a lighthouse shining over the seas of ignorance. Even as Abraham's faith was counted to him as righteousness, though far from the perfect way as we find in reading of his life, so did he win approval for his striving. But we must note that he did not "go to heaven", nor did he receive the mythical Promised Land.

So must each of us walk in the light given us for the goal that we can vision. "Prove all things; hold fast to that which is good." Such was the admonition of Apostle Paul and certainly the words hold true even in this day.

We must recognize, then, that there are as many variances in the study of religious thought as there are in the field of psychology; both studies of the soul and the mind in their respective manner. Both are striving to lead mankind to a better way of life, one through faith and one through knowledge and understanding. But neither yet possess the wisdom needed to lead man to the higher level of understanding himself, for the scientific mind does not recognize the world of spirit.

There comes that time, then, when all of the beliefs must be weighed. We dare not feel that one way of thinking and reasoning is correct and all others are incorrect, for this is nothing more than the biased mind of bigotry. Each of us must recognize the light that our neighbor has to guide him/her, and each of us must learn our own lessons in the grade we are in. We have not been appointed as judges over others; we are all neophytes, striving to find our way Home. By joining together in love we can make the journey much easier and more joyful.

Neither religion nor psychology are proven sciences, for each lacks the unequivocal evidence needed, though there is enough questionable evidence to support both. Religion brings the lay person to the position of accepting by faith that which they are taught, usually early in life, and striving to live the life so that which is promised can be the goal. Sadly, there are no facts offered, no proofs nor guarantees that it is the correct way nor that the goal they speak of even exists. It is only the knowledge and understanding which the teacher possesses that is zealously taught the people and offered as an inner hope.

In the same manner psychology also demands faith in the teacher and his/her ability to interpret that which is told them. But many do have the understanding of the different minds that we possess and how they work, oft times against one another, and therein lies the faith we have in their ability to help us. We can verify that which they claim to know. There is the feeling that more and more help will come through this type of treating the growing number of neuroses that exist as time goes on. It will not be treated as devil possessed and an exorcist called as in days past, but the problem can be identified and treated.

We are not alone in our ignorance of spiritual things. Even the Apostles who followed Jesus never quite understood his teachings. They were looking for the Messiah as spoken of in their Judaic religion, a King to rebuild their beloved Israel as supposedly promised, but not for another way of life so foreign to their Book of Torah. This is starkly revealed in the first chapter of the Book of Acts and makes us realize that they were only men with their own religious beliefs, and to change to a new idea, a new way of thinking, was as difficult for them as it is for us in this day and age.

As Jesus was with them after he reappeared, he commanded them not to depart Jerusalem yet, but to tarry for the promise of which he had told them. Acts 1:06 tells us, "When they therefore were come together, they asked of him, saying, 'Lord, wilt thou at this time restore again the kingdom of Israel?'". Even yet he was only the promised Messiah in their minds to restore the glory of their shattered government.

Only one man really understood his teachings. Surprisingly, he was not present at this gathering nor was he one of the Chosen Twelve. This was Saul of Tarsus, the persecutor of the Apostles but who later became Paul, picked by the spirit to be the apostle to the Gentile world. He was a very devout religious man. In his younger years he had been zealously taught the Torah by Gamaliel, a high priest of the Sanhedrin. This was the Book of the Law, the inner teachings of their age-old writings. Within him had been the desire to stamp out the blasphemous teachings of the new prophet, Jesus.

But, suddenly, on the road to Damascus that fateful day, it was revealed to him the meaning of the prophets and the true message in the teachings of Jesus of Nazareth whom he had persecuted.

What we don't realize today is that we do not have the true teachings of Jesus to bring us to "the perfect way". We have rituals, we have a promised salvation and a promised home in Heaven if we have faith in its teaching. But we do not have the teachings of the Father - the spirit within man - and the love of all as Jesus taught. Like the Apostles, we are waiting for the Messiah to return and build a new world, and then to "take us Home".

None of the inner teachings of Jesus were ever recorded. We have only his Beatitudes and the New Commandment that he had given his disciples, "That ye love one another as I have loved you". We have only the questionable translations of the later memoirs of his followers and the letters of Paul. We have theology and we have rituals as proclaimed by later Councils of the Medieval Church to bring forth spiritual experiences. We have song-fest and we have loud prayers of adoration to an unknown god such as we criticize in other pagan beliefs. But the needed teachings of the Way are completely missing. The true joy of revelation is lacking.

The true answers to the many questions we have propounded has never been proclaimed. They have remained hidden, except to a small minority who have sought for the deeper truths and in many cases have suffered the persecution and death this knowledge had brought.

What do we really mean when we speak of dogma and theology? We speak of these, not in a derogatory nor judging manner, but rather to show that it is literal interpretations and many paganistic rituals entwined in worshipping an anthropomorphic godhead of the mind. We mean doctrine and authoritative opinions laid down by the councils of the Roman Catholic church without verifiable proof or foundation of any kind. It was teachings forced upon the people by the early church fathers - and ordered by Emperor Constantine as the State Religion.

It has declared itself infallible, and yet its errors have been legion. This has been the greatest dividing factor the world has ever encountered, and it has tried vainly to erase every other teaching that does not agree. Certainly, it could easily fit the description of the Beast that was to arise, the Anti-Christ to enslave the people.

At the First Nicene Council in A.D.325, soon after the Roman Church was founded, it was proclaimed that the Son was of the same *substance* of Being as the Father, thereby indirectly setting limit or form to the Deity. But "God" is not *of a substance* but *is boundless* energy. With their ruling, however, God became a spirit BEING separate from man such as the earlier gods of Greece and of Rome, but with the emotions and characteristics of man. He became anthropomorphic. This was dogma, teachings that had no foundation whatsoever, nor was it in any form a new way of life.

Again, in the 5th ecumenical Council of A.D. 553 we find that it was decreed that there was no pre-existence of the soul, but that a new soul was made at every birth. It perhaps sounded very logical though it was not biblical nor with foundation. It was only a belief of the church fathers. If it were so there would be trillions of souls awaiting Judgment Day, and thousands coming every moment in ever-increasing numbers.

The deifying of Mary to be worshipped as a part of the godhead was also dogma, or doctrine, taking the place of Diana, the virgin goddess of Rome and protectors and helper of women in Roman mythology. It, too, was not biblical, but it brought woman into the church fold.

It was taught as church doctrine that the earth was the center of the universe, and that the sun and planets circled it. The belief in the miraculous creation of the earth and the fall of Adam only 6000 years ago are the very basis of this theology. Scientific studies, however, reveals our earth to be only a minute speck in the vast light-years of space, and its creation happening at least 10 million years ago. This turns the fall of Adam into nothing more than the misinterpretation of a symbolic event millions of years ago, and it makes a mockery of atonement for Adam's sin only 6000 years ago as believed.

Raymond Moyer

It is important that we realize that science is not an enemy of religion but rather another path that man has found to help him understand these mysteries that we are engulfed in. We must be aware of the important place that our intuition holds as psychological studies has shown that it has been given us as our true guide. It lies in the spirit world of thought wherein also lies the imagination that has brought forth the archetype of every imaginable thing that has been made. If it can be imagined, it can be made or done. It is within this objective part of our mind wherein lies all future forms awaiting the subjective part of the mind to make them a reality.

Our imaginative mind is nothing more than the creative spirit at work manifesting itself in the physical world. Just as a block of marble holds within itself the form of the statue hewn by the sculpture, so is our imagining mind holding the archetypes of the future, awaiting the unveiling by our actions. We could also say that within the energy of the "Big Bang" of creation contained the archetypes of all of creation, man included. This is what has been referred to as the "Mind of God".

We must assume that all of these beliefs down through time has had to be for man to see both sides of himself, the good and the bad that can prevail. We cannot have all good for there would be no overcoming and no progress. It is through trials and failures that knowledge and strength are found to endure until fulfillment comes. By the partaking of these ideas by faith alone and realizing the failure that has followed has given man the opportunity to finally realize that the carnal mind cannot fathom the spiritual ways. Only by hungrily seeking for the true knowledge will it come. Let us, then, examine the teachings we have received and seek the Path that Jesus spoke of.

130

We must then live our lives by faith in our understanding of our religion, although this does not mean with a closed mind. "Seek and ye shall find" will always be the admonition given us, and to "Prove all things", for revelations come in many ways and from the silence of meditation comes Truths. Moses found the truths for his time in "the quietness of the desert and on the mountaintop". In the same manner did Jesus find his Truths. So then must we find ours in the quietness of meditation, into the closet of our minds as Jesus proclaimed.

Thus our knowledge will continue to expand. Growth comes through change, minute though it may seem at first but expanding ever more as our light is increased. "Seek ye first the Kingdom of God, and all things (additional knowledge as needed) shall be added unto you." (Parentheses added).

The secrets of the old myths and the legends of the holy writings are revealed to the adept as wisdom and understanding comes, and with these two states of mind comes divine love. Divine love is that state of the oneness of all of creation that only wisdom and understanding of the true gospel can bring. For, from out of that one source came all forms, making it "Brotherly Love" in the true sense. That brings the desire to help and comfort all those in need of it, bringing that oneness

With these essences comes also mercy, beauty in the eye of the beholder, justice, the feeling of victory with a firm foundation, and the divine essence that brings true immortality. We realize suddenly that we are no longer finite. In the twinkling of an eye we are changed, from finite to infinite as the realization suddenly blossoms forth and we are free. "Death, where is thy sting?" For we realize in a blaze of glory that only the body "dies", and the Spirit, the "I Am", lives on, forevermore.

131

Death is only a change of bodies. Yes, we realize the body deteriorates and "dies". But the spirit body lives on, a droplet of the great ocean of Consciousness, helping to build a lake here and a river there as Wisdom and Charity draws us together. Just as the droplets of water are drawn up to form the cloud, so is the soul, the spirit, raised up for "birth" into a new body. But, as the droplet of water is still a part of the ocean, so is the soul a part of the universal consciousness.

These states of mind are not learned; they become. They must become the essence of the person who would become a spiritual leader, just as with Moses, Jesus, Paul, and even The Buddha and Mohammed. Their messages were the revelations to their followers of what was needed at that time and was one of the very essences of each man.

With the age that is now closing mankind has found that he has increased his ability to reason, and he now realizes that many things he believed were true were only illusions. All things change, we must realize that, and our understanding must also change and increase. Already we see the changes in our thoughts and in our lives even toward one another, though still far from the perfection we look for. These have come forth as a new tide washes the sands of time clean of the rubble of passing man.

The religious world has stubbornly held its ground, but the sand is being washed away from the crumbling foundations of "Theology by faith" on unfounded "Truths". The spiritual truths hidden in the bible and many other spiritual writings by words and numbers, in names of mountains and springs of water, and in the names of people are beginning to be revealed to more and more seekers who have the true desire to learn. Truth will come. With it will come change.

132

But for the moment, let us examine the view that science has provided us of the universe that streams so silently across the heavens and has attracted our ancestors for countless centuries. For therein lies the key to the interpretation of the myths of old that we hold so dear and that we are now just beginning to understand.

Let us stop and examine the fable of Adam and his fall that has supposedly cursed mankind throughout these countless generations, even the animals and the earth itself. For therein is the myth striving to explain to the people the rise of the life-force from out of world of instinct into the world of consciousness.

There was only one Tree of Life, out of which came all branches of life. "And a river went out of Eden to water the Garden, and from thence it parted and became four heads." With these directions theology has literally tried to show us where the Garden of Eden was located, where the four rivers of Chaldea join together. This certainly is a vain attempt to prove the literal story. But we are shown symbolically the four divisions from out of the Garden, first the mineral, then the plant, then the animal, and finally the Homo Sapiens. From out of the Spirit World of Eden (ether) they came, the creation of form.

So, even yet does creation come forth, from out of the Spirit World of Thought has all we see this day come. Let us open the door and gaze out into the vastness of space - and marvel at the wonders that have come from out of the Universal Mind of which we are a part.. Let us accept the revelations of science of this great wonder that has been as a sign for billions of years, from far before the infancy of mankind.

But how can we understand this great Universal Intelligence until we can understand the message written in the heavens? For within the vastness of space with its billions of spinning galaxies lies the secret behind this great, wonderful Divine Plan of the Ages.

The foundation has been laid. Now we are beginning to see and hear the travails of the birth of the Christ-Child within us. A new person is being born.

-12-

How It All Began

The story of our beginning as summarized in the first rather short chapter in the book of Genesis tells us so very little. It is really only a synopsis of how it may have happened, but with a time table that speaks of a supernatural event. Instead, we find it a mythical event, misunderstood for centuries of time. It contains only thirty-one verses to explain the creation of the universe, and especially the earth and its inhabitants. With its literal acceptance without question and its lack of explanation it is little wonder that confusion and disagreement exists.

Now, in these last days, science has given us the details to explain what is missing, for without details there can be no answer. All that has been assumed until now has been the literal interpretation of a supernatural creation of all things in a week's time - out of nothing.

Now we are shown a different meaning to the words "In the beginning . . ." We are finding through the scientific research of archeology, astronomy, chemistry, biology, and physics the "how" it could have taken place. These studies have given us an understanding of the first building blocks from which all things were made.

There is really no contradiction between science and religion. Religion has told of a beginning. Science has shown us the "how" it all happened. There is now a better understanding of the details of what was tried to be said in the analogy we have accepted as a literal historical happening. But there is still not an agreement; the Christian belief still does not accept the scientific facts as found through study and 'looking back in time". It is still taught that, "From out of nothing was all things made - in a week's time". Perhaps a little more time and patience will bridge the differences. In the meantime we must recognize that it is the inalienable right of all to belief as they choose – and all of us remain in the bonds of love.

There was a time, from about 600 B.C through 200 B.C., during the ancient days of the Grecian empire when man concluded that all things were made from four primary elements, earth, air, fire, and water. This truly was a giant step upward in his intelligence, and it revealed that he was searching for an answer to the many mysteries that filled his world. He had already learned the control and use of fire, and had even charted the heavens above him with his very meager instruments. Writing, in its crude forms, had also been invented only a few centuries before. But during this Grecian era his knowledge took a quantum leap forward, both in philosophy and in scientific studies.

This meager conclusion of the primary elements continued until the 5th century B.C. when another Grecian named Emedocles announced that these four primary elements were not primary after all, but were really only different manifestations or molecules of ONE primary element.

We can only imagine how this revelation was accepted since we have seen many new ideas flounder for a century or more for even a small acceptance. It took many centuries before man believed that the earth was round and that it circled the sun. But this new announcement agreed in principal with the Ageless Wisdom taught in the Mystery Schools of that day in which Socrates, Plato, and many other brilliant minds attended.

It revealed that the scientific mind was awakening.

With the discovery within this last century of the many galaxies that exists in space, they also found that the universe was expanding at quite a tremendous rate, and was turning. This startling fact raised the theory that at some distant time in the past all matter had to be gathered together in the same place at the same time. There was a beginning. Out of this theory has come another theory, that of "The Big Bang" of creation billions of years ago.

This is explained by Dr. Harry Shipment, assistant professor of astronomy at the University of Delaware (pp.230) in his book, "Black Holes, Quasars, and the universe."

"The story starts," he wrote, "with a homogeneous glob of matter containing all the substance of the universe. This glob was hot and dense . . . in the form of a number of minute particles with exotic names . . . along with the more familiar names such as protons, neutrons, electrons and photons." These are only bits and pieces which make up atoms of form.

In a previous page (pp.229) he tells of this concentrated single lump, the primeval atom, and how it exploded to create the motion that is still expanding the universe.

Now we have the picture more firmly in our minds of the possibility of how it all began. Here we have the beginning of the violence that we have seen scattered throughout the universe. Particles this hot and this dense "glob" collided a million times a second until, with a giant flash of light, a nuclear reaction took place, sending radiation and energy particles far into space at incredible speeds - and as cooling began, fusion of particles begins to form matter.

This is what science says that possibly did happen, in one giant nuclear explosion, throwing white-hot neutrons and protons and electrons and everything else (except the kitchen sink) out into the extremely cold emptiness of space.

"And God said, 'Let there be light, and there was light'" (Genesis 1:3). Possibly more than He expected!

Then began the cooling and the forming. First it was only hydrogen with its one atom, but after the first twenty minutes of slightly cooling, it became one-quarter helium and the residue still only minute particles of . . . something called radiation which much of it still remains and is being captured in our giant radio antennas scattered throughout the world.

Just how long ago did this happen? How long before Columbus discovered the New World, you might ask. How long before the pyramids were built? How long before man broke free from the trees? How long before the earth was formed? We must go much farther back than that.

We can see that questions abound that we have never thought of before; space and stars and galaxies as having a beginning. We have been told that they were just miraculously put there in the heavens on the third day of creation, one day AFTER the earth was created.

Science, however, does tell us that the Big Bang happened approximately fifteen BILLION years ago! We can hardly imagine such a period of time; it was hardly "only yesterday." It certainly was more than the six thousand years as claimed by our religious theology, or 4004 B.C. as has have claimed.

Seemingly, the first creation were great clouds of the gases which in turn formed the suns that later became quasars as the laws of gravity, cohesion and adhesion became affective to begin the formation of matter. Quasars, we find, are the remnants of these first suns and are now the most luminous objects in the universe, super massive clouds of glowing gases that are still extremely hot, as explained by James Grant in the Science Magazine, July, 1995, "flooding the early universe with the energy of hundreds of billions of suns".

These distant quasars were first discovered by radio astronomers because of their very powerful emissions of radio waves of energy. Finally, in knowing just where to look, astronomers found them, just tiny red-like dots in the far reaches of space.

In viewing them billions of light years away, we are looking back billions of years in time, seeing a pattern of the beginning of creation. Again Robert and Sarah Williams Scherrer explains, "Here a barrier exists that prevents us from looking all the way back to the birth of time. It is an opaque curtain . . set by the very particles of matter from which the universe grew . . that no telescope can pierce."

The first stars (suns) were created as large amounts of the gases cooled and in turn these particles were drawn into a mass by gravitational force. This slow contraction as "in the beginning" caused the atoms to collide more and more with each other and the gases heated. Eventually, the gases became so hot that the atoms no longer bounced off each other, but rather coalesced to form helium, releasing tremendous amounts of energy. A star is born. This energy released is a continuing nuclear furnace, much the same as a hydrogen bomb exploding continuously and it is this light that makes the star shine.

Billions more formed as time went on, and gravity pulled them into the galaxies that the astronomers now study. In the meantime, suns within these galaxies are also dying as their fuel is spent, changing as it cools from hydrogen to helium to carbon, and then finally to the heavier metals we find in our own earth. The glowing suns turns into "white dwarfs" or "neutron stars", according to their density.

Sometimes, however, the outer regions of these dying suns would be blown off in a tremendous explosion called a supernova, a blast outshining all other suns in its galaxy. The heavier metals formed in these last stages. Iron, lead, nickel, gold, etc., would be blown off into space to become the dust and debris that will again coalesce to form the next sun or possibly a planet such as ours.

This does not end the intense activity but rather begins anew the building of other forms for the eventual tearing apart once more. Dr. Shipman, in his book "Black Holes, Quasars, and the Universe" mentioned earlier, also tells of the forming of black holes out of collapsing suns and the finality of being caught in their gravitational pull.

An article in the July, 1995 issue of the Scientific American magazine, however, told of some physicists doubting their existence. "I don't believe in black holes," declares Phillip Morrison, a physicist at M. I. T. This shows us that many theories exist about space and its objects, but there also can be a great amount of disagreement before a theory becomes a fact. But disagreement is good, for it assures that all angles, all ideas, and all proofs will be examined, and out of this theory will come a proven fact - for our day.

We do hear that black holes are being "discovered" with numbing regularity these days, according to the above article and many other astronomers. A number of them, writing an article in Nature magazine, even stated that many galaxies are thought to contain massive black holes at their centers. Firm evidence has proven to be elusive, however, but the observing of the gases and suns rotating very rapidly around a central body is rather compelling evidence to many that such a massive black hole might possibly exist.

What this means to us is that there can exist a devouring something, regardless of its name, that is so dense and containing such a gravitational pull that other forms of energy can be trapped within it, even waves of light that is bent inward so that they can no longer be seen. We know that light waves can be bent by passing through a prism. Can they also be bent enough by the pull of gravity to reverse their direction? And this energy, being tightly pressed, cannot be destroyed. Another problematic question that some day will have to be answered.

This thought makes us hope with all our heart and mind that Captain Kirk can steer the USS Enterprise away from such a catastrophic place. We will be watching the ensuing episodes of Star Trek with far more interest from now on.

Now we are realizing that there is a Universal Consciousness of boundless energetic powers that is creating and destroying throughout space in an effort to become manifest in form. It is Boundless Energy and Limitless Light (Wisdom). The concept of a great Spirit BEING called "God" watching over this tiny speck in the arm of one of billions of galaxies becomes nothing more than another myth created in the mind of man to coincide with his other myths. We find Jehovah nothing more than a

141

mythical Hebrew race god to answer their need for a deity. The "Father" is unknowable with our mini understanding and the warped guidance that we have received from theology down through these centuries of time. But the dawn is coming to reveal these mysteries as science replaces superstitions and religion with facts and reality.

There are other myths told in other age-old writings such as the Vedas and Upanishads of the early Aryans of India that hint of a truer understanding. They tell of the Father/Mother, the binary positive and negative, resting in the quietness of infinite, formless space, and "Darkness alone filled the Boundless All". Then came the outbreath of the Mother and the first Logos (Motion) was created. It is sad that all these myths of old could not have been brought forth to give mankind a more realistic picture in his mind of the beginning of time and motion.

So, as we stand here on earth alongside a Texas road looking up into the sky and seeing all the beautiful stars shining back at us, and the graceful expanse of the Milky Way, we can begin to visualize the meaning of all the old stories that have been hidden from us - by Church Fathers. We can assure our lovers that all is not as it seems. Violence is hidden by light years of space. Suns are dying in great explosions, and matter is being swallowed by giant black holes. Some day even our sun will fail and go out or explode, though luckily time is on our side. Our concern at the moment is to assure our lover that our love will last longer than the stars, eternally.

We still have another million or more years of sunlight left. Then, ". . . Darkness was upon the face of the deep" will be the Omega of earth and its inhabitants. (Genesis 1:2).

Time - and man - will be no more . . . . . .

-13-

The Violent Universe

"The heavens declare the glory of God; and the firmament showeth his handi-work."

This was the realization of King David as he gazed mystified up into the black abyss and saw the wonder of wonders above him. So do we of today still gaze in awe into the vast unknown above us, though few there are that realize the violence that is hidden by distance from all but the seeking astrologers and cosmologists.

How, then, can a man/woman ever begin to know the glory of God until they, too, have gazed deep into the immensity of the heavens and tried to understand how such could be? Is it not surprising to finally discover the knowledge that the ancient adepts seemed to possess when we realize they had no telescopes or computers, but only their naked eyes to study the heavens. We can only vision them lying for many hours under the stars as they tended their flocks, striving to understand the mysteries of it all. It is a wonder far above all wonders.

"His going forth is from the end of heaven, and His circuit unto the ends of it."

How great a circuit is this? We have gazed out into space over 15 Billion LIGHT YEARS and still have not reached the end, or rather the beginning. When we consider a light year to be over 5.8 trillion miles; we haven't even a name for a distance of 15 billion times 5.8 trillion miles, and we haven't yet seen to the very edge. Can it really have been that all of this grandeur was scattered above us in only the hours contained in the fourth day of creation? Or can it be that we have been mis-informed by the translation of the facts laid before us?

Let's take a moment and gaze up into the sky again, this time with an open heart and an open mind. It is imperative that we understand the universe as the Body of God so that we can recognize God. We must understand Creation in its fullness so that we can understand the Creator.

This twentieth century has been the time when man finally was able to push aside the bonds of scientific ignorance and open the window to this vast, unknown universe. Turning from our religious beliefs to empirical studies he began to probe the mysteries that stretched far beyond what his naked eyes could ever hope to reach for a better understanding of his place in the Big Picture of Creation.

Aiming his telescopes and great listening devises in the direction of faint radio signals and gazing deep into the mysterious blackness he discovered a faint speck of light over 15 billion light years away. It was a quasar, the remnants of a star over 15 billion years old. It told that the light from it had been traveling for, lo, these billions of years, at a speed of 186,000 miles per SECOND, and only then was it reaching earth.

This door was opened in 1924 when Edwin Hubble made the astounding discovery that the universe contained not only our galaxy as presumed but countless others. It was the beginning of the lid being removed from outer space as distance began to be measured not in miles but in light years. Soon after, in 1929, Hubble made another astounding discovery by finding that the universe was expanding. Suddenly, the sky above was far different than had ever been imagined. Soon, billions of galaxies were discovered, each filled with its own billions of suns very similar to our own but of varying sizes. Imagine, if at all possible, billions upon billions of nuclear furnaces similar to our own sun streaming across the heavens, shining out for our eyes to see!

Each galaxy stretched out in distances again measurable only in thousands of light years, an astronomical figure that even yet our minds cannot begin to fathom. Gigantic clouds of dust and gases floated in the midst of the suns, remnants of earlier exploding suns and the building blocks of new ones.

A completely new concept of God's kingdom began to unfold. Our place in His total creation became only a minute blue speck situated in one of the arms of the galaxy that we see sweeping across our heavens, the Milky Way. No longer were we the stationary center of the universe and the great importance that we have claimed for the many centuries of inner vanity, but in actuality hardly even a speck in the eye of the Creator.

Science in its endeavors to broaden our knowledge has turned space from an expanse of heavenly splendor as believed since the dawn of time into a violent, unending workplace of a formless yet energetic consciousness continually building and destroying to build a new, more advanced form of matter. The window of the vastness of space had finally been opened to the common man and has broadened the mind from an earth-and-heaven concept to the realization that the True Deity that we so ignorantly worshipped these many centuries is creative energy with limitless possibilities of creativeness. It has brought a dramatic change to the religious thinking of many so that the God of a spirit BEING on a heavenly throne has faded into the realization that "God" is only a mythical title, a symbol of that which we don't understand. Now we realize it to be the universal expression of energy. The latent energy of Chaos, "Before the Beginning", had become kinetic (usable) energy (work) manifested in the creation of form.

This is a far cry from the God of theology that creates things instantaneously out of nothing and does miraculous, almost unbelievable things in the same manner. But things just don't happen that way, except in myths and fairy tales. The sun doesn't stop at a man's command, nor does an ocean part to allow people to escape. There must be a cause and an explanation for all things. There is rhythmic order in the universe with its immutable laws to govern, for without it there would be the chaos as found in the domain of man.

From out of the ancient wisdom of Greece has come the adage that whatever comes to be must come from what already is, for where else could it have come? It almost makes sense, doesn't it? Why could not I have thought of so simple an explanation?

We must realize at first that the sun doesn't revolve around the earth; we circle it. It doesn't rise nor set. Every twenty-four hours the earth turns every point of its face to the sun. It would be catastrophic for the earth to suddenly stop, or even to hesitate even for an instant as it travels over 1000 miles per hour in its exacting path.

We realize that phenomenon happen that we don't understand but we can be assured that universal laws govern and that the answer to these mysteries will come as it always does to those who truly seek for truth. We know little about the influence of passing comets and the collisions of asteroids that we know have struck the earth and our moon, and of the many catastrophes by earthquake and volcanic explosions that have happened, but we also must realize everything is the result of some cause.

As we begin to understand the universe we begin to realize what "In the beginning" really meant. We begin to understand the creation of all stars and galaxies and quasars, what a nebulae is, and even how our earth came into existence. This is not a new heresy; this was known in ancient times. Now we are opening our minds that were closed by our early religious leaders to facts laid before us to weigh against old beliefs. It is stepping back from the world of superstition and myths and examining the new evidence laid before us. It is the opening of this new era with 21st century thinking and reasoning. It is also helping us to understand what the ancient myths were trying to relate.

Imagine for a moment of stopping along the highway on the broad flat prairie-land of West Texas, or perhaps along a flat Kansas wheat-field. It is night, and dark. The moon has not yet appeared. The lights of cities and towns are barely visible on the distant horizon. A peaceful quietness engulfs us as we stand there gazing upward into the dark unknown and marvel.

Looking up into the darkness we see a sky filled with uncountable dots of light. But we only see the heavens just above our part of the earth.

We could perhaps wonder about the other directions that we never see. Are they, too, streaked in gigantic patterns of stars, or suns, as your own heavens? Are we somewhere in the midst of a grandeur so vast that even our imagination fails miserably to vision it?

In the darkened sky far above we would see millions of stars forming our galaxy called The Milky Way. These stars are actually other suns such as our own as we now realize. Perhaps they, too, have formed solar systems similar to ours and perhaps someone on a planet out there just might be looking out towards us with the same wonderment as we.

Seemingly at rest, all of these suns, including ours, are spiraling around the center of this galaxy as our planets spiral around our sun. We find that our planet is only a minute speck circling one of the billions of suns that form this galaxy that we are gazing at all around us.

Stephen Hawking, a brilliant astronomer of our day, in his book, "A Brief History Of Time", explains this expanding universe in a manner that is astounding in its simplicity. We begin to understand the possibility of the "How" it all began. It is a concept of utter immensity that our imagination cannot begin to conceive. Now we must rely on the astronomer, the geologists and the geophysicists to tell us the rest of the story. Certainly it will change somewhat as more and more information is discovered, but for us now it is the only records we have of the mysteries of the unknown past.

The reality that the Milky Way is over 100,000 LIGHT YEARS across is also farther than the human mind can fathom, especially when we try to realize the trillions of miles in only one light year. The fact that our sun and its solar system, along with over 200 BILLION other suns, are actually a part of this huge galaxy streaming across the heavens is truly incomprehensible. Then we must try to realize that we - and our entire solar system - is located in one of its giant arms with other suns.

So we finally realize that our tiny planet is lost in the immensity of the creation that has unfolded since the Big Bang. But what we see is only a small part of the true BIG picture. These several BILLIONS of galaxies are also in great clusters throughout the universe, with from 25 to over 1000 of these giant galaxies in each cluster, and we still have not seen an end, or edge. This makes us shrink even smaller in this Body of God called the Universe, and we should hang our head in shame for the centuries of thinking how important we were in such a creation.

Only in this day are we beginning to grasp the vastness and the tremendous violence that goes on before our very eyes, though unseen because of distance. Yes, this is the workshop of the Great Creativeness in the center of every atom that we have called God. We have failed miserably in our conception of this Supreme Intelligence, for we have strived to contain "It" into a Spirit BEING that made - and lost - us and place "it" in a position high above us in a nebulous Heaven. Only until we understand the universe and its ever-changing pattern from "In the beginning" can we ever hope to conceive the true Creative Intelligence.

Only now can we begin to understand what Brahma, Vishnu, and Siva, the three gods of their trinity, meant in the Hindu mythology. Brahma represents the creative principal, Vishnu is the preserver, the sender of the avatars to educate, and Siva is the destroyer to build again. Yet they are of one essence, from out of the One, formless entity of energy.

The Trinity of the West is very similar. We have the Father, the Universal Binary Intelligence, the Son, the creative force of motion, and the Holy Ghost, that Unconsciousness within each of us to guide us. This latter is also referred to as the Comforter, for as we seek answers it opens the door of our mind to understanding.

The interest and study of the stars dates back into a time when man first became aware of his surroundings. There is really no known date except to say that it was in the dawn of civilization, thousands of years ago. From that time there began the realization that certain patterns of the sun and the moon brought certain happenings to his environment in regular rotation. These were the seasons. Putting these patterns of the stars together formed the constellations, which in turn became the zodiac that our solar system seems to travel through in its circular track through space. From this meager knowledge man learned to plan his life.

The Egyptians seemingly were the first recorded race to develop this knowledge into their culture, for it allowed them to know in advance the time of flooding by the Nile. When the sun was in a certain constellation of the zodiac each year, the floods came. Soon thereafter came the planting time. This we can see was the beginning of astrology, how the movement of the stars affected their lives. The alignment of massive stones in England called Stonehenge showed more than a passing interest in the sun and the stars even as early as 3000 BC in another part of the world. It was perhaps one of the first ancient observatories built for that purpose where the priests could follow the annual motion of the sun in order to predict the seasons and where they no doubt worshipped.

The study of the heavens became more of a science in ancient Babylon and Chaldea from roughly 1800 B.C. to 400 B.C. with the actual charting of the sky and the phases of the moon that brought about the first calendar. Cuneiform tablets found and deciphered within this last century have shown an extreme degree of accuracy for their meager instruments. Later came the realization that certain patterns of the stars brought other happenings and it became a near science.

These early studies were the beginning of what we now term astronomy, the scientific study of the celestial bodies to develop theories that will explain the origin, evolution, and possibly the destiny of the universe. It has grown to include many fields of study, such as radio, infrared, and radar astronomy, studying even the thousands of waves of energy emitted from space that bombard our planet.

During these many intervening centuries there has been different theories of the universe. This was pointed out by Robert and Sarah Williams Scherrer in the November, 1995 issue of Astronomy. "The search for our beginnings is a quest that has occupied the activities of scientists for thousands of years . . ." They told of the great curtain of ignorance pulled over the universe, much the same as the ignorance of our own world in centuries past. "Explorers, both cosmic and earthly," they continued, "have frequently encountered such curtains . . ."

The Scherrers went on to show how long this curtain of ignorance had remained. "It is almost unbelievable that even until this 20th century many rather well-known astronomers believed that the stars in the Milky Way comprised the entire universe. Only in the 1920's when Edwin Hubble measured the distances to nearby galaxies did astronomers push back their "curtains of ignorance." We do not think of our sciences as being controlled by narrow beliefs, but we find that they, too, are only fragile men.

This is an astounding fact of how even learned individuals will hold fast to their beliefs even though many proofs are laid at their feet. It is the example of the fragility of faith not founded upon proven facts. Even great knowledge does not make change any easier to accept. It is as the old adage states, "Don't try to confuse me with facts. My mind is already made up."

The greatest misconception of man and his universe has been the belief that the earth has been the ultimate creation of God and the heavens has been the ceiling. Aristotle of early Greece (384 - 322 B.C.), summarized this with his geocentric theory that the earth was stationary and the sun and planets circled the earth. This made the earth the center of the universe.

In his writings, Aristotle stated that the earth was "at rest" and everything revolved around it. Surprisingly, it remained the consensus of many renowned astronomers until this very century, and of course it is still believed by the masses (who really care less) who are taught by the theology of the churches that we are the ultimate creation of "God". We have found only recently that our sun and its solar system is also circling the center of the Milky Way as it, too, circles through space around the center of the giant cluster of which it is a part.

To confound man's thinking even more in those early days, Ptolemy (100 - 165 A.D.), in his search for answers, created a model of the solar system, which seemingly proved this geocentric theory. It was not a perfect model for the paths of the planets are not perfect circles as he supposed. This was the accepted theory, however, and was taught in the early Roman church and its universities for centuries. It coincided with their belief that the earth and man were the ultimate creation of God in the center of His Heavenly domain.

Thankfully, man has never been content with a theory until it has been proven to be true. It may take years, or even centuries. But time, being relative, means little in his quest for knowledge, for eventually he will learn. Then he can have faith that what he knows is a proven fact.

In the meantime, the universe continues to expand from that instant 15 billion years ago when it exploded into being. "And God said, 'Let there be light, and there was light'".

But that is another story to be told around the campfires at another time.

-14-

The Universe Discovered

It is important that we look back into history at times to see what the way of thinking was compared to what our understanding is at this moment in time. It shows us in a dramatic way that man's mind is continually expanding as we compare our previous knowledge with the present revelations that have come forth. It is the acceptance of new ideas, though reluctant at times perhaps, that brings the progress and changes that we have enjoyed throughout this long history.

So, once again we gather around the campfire of old and wait as the Shaman stares into the flickering flames. Finally, he raises his eyes heavenward and begins to speak, slow and deliberate, as if each word must be carefully chosen.

"There was a time, so very long ago, when there was nothing, before even time existed . . . . . ."

The book of Genesis is being literally revealed before our very eyes, just as it was a thousand centuries ago. We realize that even then the mind of man reached back into the depth of his intuition for the answers to the mysteries surrounding him, just as we, today, are reaching out for ours.

It is hard to realize that it was only yesterday, relative speaking, that even the scientific world believed that the sun and its other planets circled our motionless earth! Superstitions abounded. The earth was supposedly supported by water, although someone had remarked rather briskly that everyone should realize that it was supported by turtles, all the way to the bottom.

Only 2500 years ago the earth was considered flat. Ships venturing too far at sea might fall off the edge into oblivion. Barely 600 years ago witches were burned at the stake to destroy the evil spirits in our own early colonies. This is truly proof of how slowly the evolution of man and his knowledge has been down through the many ages of time that he has been on this earth. Only now are we beginning to realize the many superstitions that were hidden in our religions down through time.

As we stated previously, the Grecian, Aristotle, conceived this geocentric theory of the sun and planets circling the earth about 350 B.C. It was nearly 1900 years later before the true path was realized, and even then it was believed by only a few until the twentieth century, our own time in history.

The heliocentric theory, that the earth and planets revolved around the sun, came from the mind of a Polish priest and Church mathematician named Nicholas Copernicus. This was in 1514 A.D., only slightly less than five hundred years ago.

Both the Church and the scientific world were shocked at what Copernicus claimed. Both heaped scorn upon him and his work. Had not the great minds of Aristotle and Ptolomy swore that the geocentric theory was correct? Had not Ptolemy himself devised a model that proved it beyond a shadow of a doubt? (But his model showed the planets moving in perfect circles around the earth.)

Copernicus could present no proof except his paper and his figures. The telescope had not yet been invented. For this heresy he was excommunicated from the Church and placed under house arrest by the Roman government, which in reality was one and the same. Sadly, he died in shame soon after.

Before he died, Copernicus wrote, "If the earth is the center of the universe and the center of God's creation, then man on earth might well be one of the greatest objects of God's care. But, if my theory is right, and the earth is but one of many planets revolving in space, and not even the largest of them, then this earth upon which we live and the men upon it may not be as important in God's scheme as we have imagined."

This theory was believed and supported about a century later by another mathematician named Galileo who saw the planets moving through space through the first telescope. This invention allowed him to plot the path of each around the sun, and he saw a universe much larger than had ever been imagined.

The Church still banned the theory of Copernicus for it contradicted the Bible which they had translated and printed. Galileo was ordered to deny his findings to remain faithful to the Church, though he later wrote a book that explained both theories without taking sides.

The book was received as a masterpiece, but Galileo was again forced to publicly denounce the teachings of Copernicus. He, too, was put under house arrest for life.

Even under these harsh conditions by his Church, he knew his book was correct and that he was wrong to denounce it. He wrote another book, "Two New Sciences", that was smuggled to Holland and in time became the start of modern Physics. He died ten years later, still under house arrest and condemned by his church.

Another young astronomer named Johannes Kepler joined Galileo in the support of this new theory. Though quite young, he was trained in mathematics and philosophy, as well as theology. At the age of 24 he wrote and published "The Cosmographic Mystery" in which he defended the Copernicus theory. Soon after, other astronomers began accepting this idea as the newly invented telescope showed its truth.

The sky, however, from this 16th century world of Galileo and Kepler until this 20th century remained only the Milky Way and a few thousand other stars, or suns. It seemed a closed system. The scientific world reluctantly accepted the new heliocentric theory, but very few other new theories were brought out in those early years, and lovers were left to gaze at the heavenly splendor and marvel at its beauty as they pleased.

The door to the universe was opened slightly by the discoveries of Edwin Hubble. Countless galaxies existed, he discovered, rather than just our own Milky Way. But the masses cared little about space; they were building a materialistic, democratic, religious society here on this planet with the help and guidance of God.

Then, suddenly it happened. The jolting awareness of outer space came on a day in 1957 when a tiny Russian satellite named Sputnik orbited the earth to open the door for the masses to a completely new and baffling world. Television caught this fever and for the next few years kept us highly informed of space with dramatic pictures of orbiting capsules and finally the ultimate story and pictures of the actual landing on the moon.

Since World War II there had been a growing interest in the importance of space for our security. The sudden impact of Sputnik on October 4, 1957 was the true wake-up call to our nation, and especially so when two additional sputniks were launched soon after. The second was launched on November 3, 1957, carrying with it a passenger, a dog named Laika. A short time later, on May 15, 1958, the third sputnik blasted off and again almost tauntingly circled above us. We were a shocked and frightened nation.

Television increased this awareness. It strove to comfort us by the dramatic pictures of our own orbiting capsules, and finally, our actual landing on the moon. None of these, however, had the impact and the captured audience that the fictional flights of the Spaceship USS Enterprise of the television series, "Star Trek". This caught the intense interest in space travel. This, above all other stories, showed our planet as only a tiny dot in a vast, uncharted universe of distant galaxies. New names of outer worlds and "warped speed" entered our vocabulary as, in our imagination, we visited unknown planets with strange life forms in other parts of space, and surprisingly, they all spoke English.

In the early '60's our president, John F. Kennedy, began our space program in earnest, and our pledge to be the first on the moon became a reality. Apollo Eleven blasted off July 16, 1969 and arrived on the moon July 20th to thrust the first flag into the surface. That was truly a day of celebration and pride that America needed in its troubled times.

From that day forward space became an important study. Rocket launches were a common occurrence, and even space probes were sent out among the planets with little fan-fare. The first successful probe was Mariner 2, launched August 27, 1962, and passed to within 21,000 miles of Venus. Other Mariner probes followed, studying each of the inner planets, Mercury, Venus and Mars.

Then came the Voyager probes, as Voyager 1 blasted off from Kennedy Space Center in Florida on December 5, 1977 to visit the planet Jupiter. Surprisingly, Voyager 2 was launched first, on August 20, 1977, for it was to take a longer trajectory to the same planet. After both visited Jupiter and Uranus, they were then turned toward outer space and the unknown, both carrying records and pictures for whoever might intercept them. But as they flew away, Voyager 1 turned her cameras one more time to our solar system and took a "family portrait" of the sun and its planets. The planets were so widespread that it required Voyager to snap 60 different pictures to include them all.

Lee Dye, of the L.A. Times-Washington Post Service wrote of The Voyagers' final series. ". . capturing the planets of the solar system just as they were intended to be seen - as insignificant points of light in a dark, cold universe".

Carl Sagan, the well-known astronomer and writer, remarked when he saw the mosaic that had been created, "This is where we live," pointing to a tiny dot among the others, "on this tiny blue dot." He summed it up by adding, "Now it (Voyager 1) is speeding out toward outer space, . . . making it possible for it to take this one last look over its shoulder as it plunges into the inter-stellar dark."

But none of these studies and probes ever picked up the radar blip of the USS Enterprise with Captain Kirk at the helm, still shooting through the heavens at "warp speed". It shows that the mind and imagination of man is still far ahead of the actual knowledge, but this is what leads us deeper into the unknown. First there must be the thought, the archetype. Perhaps he and Buck Rogers will meet some day on a distant planet and talk over times that we may someday know.

Astronomy had come of age in the twentieth century. It is now looking out into unending space and beginning to understand what it sees. Edwin Hubble's discovery in 1924 opened a new era of study by demonstrating that ours was not the only galaxy, but rather billions of others were scattered throughout the universe. He had devised a method of determining the distance to visible stars by their color and brightness, making it possible to separate the different galaxies. This brought the revelation that the universe was expanding as the distances increased between them just as the spots on a balloon as it is inflated.

The discovery of an expanding universe was truly one of the great intellectual discoveries of the twentieth century. The day of revelation had definitely arrived, for science and for mankind alike, and definitely for those astronomers who had devoted their life's work to this one cause.

Another factor leading to this vast amount of new knowledge in these times is the modern instruments that became available. On our Mount Palomar near Los Angeles, California, is the great 200-inch reflecting telescope continually searching the heavens, and on Mt. Wilson overlooking Los Angeles is another, though smaller telescope. Countless others are scattered at many strategic locations throughout the world. All of these, with the great number of radio telescopes with their huge dishes or ears pointed to the many areas of the sky being studied, have increased knowledge a thousand-fold.

What has man seen out there? A heavenly domain? A dark, mysterious expanse of beautiful stars? Far more than that. He has seen exploding suns, giant clouds of deadly gases called nebulae, collisions of galaxies, and signs of quasars and mysterious black holes. He has seen, in these exploding suns, the nuclear fusion that has formed the very elements of matter that has formed our earth.

Though such a peaceful and glorious sight exists from the viewpoint of the average citizen along a Texas or Kansas roadside, the astronomer sees a universe of incredible heat and deadly radiation, with violent explosions and collisions beyond human imagination.

This is the reality that is before us. We can be assured that all was not created in a single week some 6000 years ago; it has taken eons of time to build what we see today from the minute particles of energy from that first moment of time. Let us not take as long to accept and enjoy it.

-15-

The Story Continues

There comes a time in a child's life when the realization comes that the fairy tales that lulled them to sleep were written not only to entertain them, but within these stories was a hidden message to teach an early truth.

The story of the little toy train called, "The Little Engine Who Tried" had its message. It taught the lesson of continued effort for success in our endeavors. "I think I can, I think I can, I KNOW I CAN!" Another of these fairy tales, "The Three Little Pigs", taught to build solid dreams so that the winds of fate cannot destroy them.

It was an ingenious method of teaching lessons in a happy captivating way so that children would never tire of hearing them time and again. In turn, the messages would be ingrained deep within their subconscious through repetition, for it is through repetition that memory and knowledge are built and learned.

But there comes a time when these mythical stories must be laid aside and the books of deeper learning must be opened.

Our schooling in the ways of life and growth must also begin at some moment in our life as we begin to reason for ourselves. We must learn to accept the proven facts of progressive knowledge and the voice of our intuition as it strives to separate the truth from the chaff, even though it may be against the accepted teachings of the past.

We are at a turning point for the masses now, much the same as we reached for the leaders of the people twenty one centuries ago. The theological world was shown by the infant scientific world of Copernicus and Galileo that the earth was not the center of the universe as believed so vehemently, and that the sun and planets did not rotate around us. But the leaders and teachers of that day which were of the medieval Roman Church held tenaciously to their fables. They tried to erase this new knowledge by punishing those that dared conceive it and kept the trusting masses in ignorance of these great truths. In reality, these teachings and the teachings of creation should have been questioned and corrected centuries ago.

Since that time knowledge has increased a thousand-fold. In the western world the masses has been freed from the threats of both Church and State and the day of reasoning has come to the fore. We can vote for our leaders of government, though the people are still vulnerable by the words of politicians who promise "the moon" to be elected. We can choose our religion, though none are the perfect Way as yet. We can partially choose our own pathway in life, though few have found the more perfect path given us to follow.

But the spiritual light is beginning to shine so that all who seek it are free to weigh all things both in the religious and the scientific worlds and to choose which way we want to go. What a wonderful time to be alive! Yet, we still must come to the realization that the time his arrived when the myths are being unveiled and each of us must be responsible for the seeds we sow - and the stories we accept.

It is important for us to realize that the scientific world has shown us that the sun and the moon and the earth didn't just happen supernaturally in seven short days as we have been taught. "In the beginning" was a few billion years ago. Heaven is not a place just above us in the clouds that we have sung about, but rather a state of mind. Space has suddenly become a vastness of billions of galaxies and distances measurable only in light years, and our deity is not just above us on a heavenly throne.

Sadly, many still refute these new thoughts. The blame must be put squarely upon the shoulders of theology who still teach the age-old beliefs of the past and frighten the people with the threat of eternal fire. But we must recognize that it is not for any of us to set the standards of what people believe, for this responsibility is upon each individual as his inalienable right, and each must reach out and seek a higher understanding as their season comes.

The divine responsibility of our leaders has now reached the point where these fairytales must end and the true knowledge of man and his place in this vast universe must be explained. Why are we here? Where did we come from to be born here on this earth? Is amassing fortunes our ultimate goal? and, most important of all, do we have the right to ask such question?

We could truthfully say that we are here to assist the Universal Consciousness to reach its ultimate goal of Perfection. But that is nebulous.

Perhaps we could say that we are here, with the talents and knowledge each of us have, to help creation evolve to its potentials.

We came from out of this Universal Consciousness eons ago as a branch on the Tree of Life. We have been striving upward ever since. Amassing fortunes and gaining power over others is nothing more than vanity in a finite world. It is our duty to ourselves and to society that we strive for a better understanding of these same questions, and strive for a more perfect way than what we have built.

As we study the myths and the legends of all the races of mankind we find the same hidden messages deep within each of them. They, too, were told and eventually read over and over to the people so that their beginnings would be ingrained deep within their subconscious. These are the stories of Creation, the story of Noah, of Moses, of Krishna, of Guatama the Buddha, and of Jesus. Each has its own variations, and, of course, each has its own name for the Characters portrayed, and the avatars have come to each race to lead the people onward.

Surprisingly, when all are heard and analyzed, all are in very close agreement. This is the undeniable proof that there is a something within all of us that yearns for an understanding of the unknown powers of the universe, that which each of us names as a deity, and that every race has searched for it. But only one, the Judaic-Christian legend has striven to set its name of the deity and an age on creation as the ultimate truth, and to draw all other races to this one belief.

The western world of Christianity has accepted the Hebrew version of Creation as told in the bible as the true, literal story above all others, presumably written by Moses. It has never been questioned throughout the long, passing centuries, but has been accepted as "God's Holy Word". This story, however, is believed to have been copied by Ezra and his scribes from the older writings of Chaldea during the years of the captivity of the Israelites in Babylon, for their own writings had been destroyed by the destruction of Jerusalem by their captors.

This does not distract one iota from its concept of creation, though it does allow us to examine it in a different light, the light of reason, for the message it contains. We find its source from a different race - and a different God - than portrayed to us.

Words have many meanings. Unfold means to open and spread out; it also means to reveal. Spring means a season; it also means a source of water, a coiled piece of steel, etc. Day means a period of 24 hours, a period of time in history, an era.

The word translated as Day was taken from the Hebrew as "aeon" in the Greek version but was later translated into English as Day. So, our belief in the timing of "in the beginning" has been founded upon the very interpretation of ONE WORD, that of DAY. This changed it from an evolving creation over an era of time which Genesis does allow through translation to a sudden, supernatural occurrence that happened in only seven literal days as theology swears. One could easily mutter, "Preposterous!" for every minute detail to have been accomplished in such a short time, just as they are today, even supernaturally.

Another word that has caused much confusion is the word translated as Adam. The Hebrew account does not refer to this as one man but as a generic word. Nor does the earlier Chaldean records from whence it possibly could have come. Both use it as a more generalized way of speaking of early mankind. Even Plato, in his Symposium spoke of original mankind as of globular form and androgynous until separated into male and female.

This coincides with the bible version, "male and female made He them", and agrees also with the findings of science.

In the scientific studies of our earth we find different periods of development called ages as we have shown earlier, when certain drastic changes came about. The forming of the earth itself, with the seas and the continents, were in what was called the Pre-Cambrian era. This was a steaming, hot, life-less era of early formation in preparation for the first microscopic organisms to form from the amino acids, the building blocks of life, in the warm waters during the next, the Paleozoic era. The third, the Mesozoic era, brought life-forms from out of the waters onto dry land to form the air-breathing creatures as the fauna began producing the necessary oxygen. Then, 70 million years or so ago, began the Cenozoic era wherein the animals that we now recognize came forth, and also the branch of primitive man. This is what is termed the evolution of life-forms over millions of years, seemingly a great stumbling block for the theological world of Creationism..

If we can accept that creation happened over a period of eons of time instead of the instantaneous manner by an anthropomorphic God, a Spirit Being as taught, then we can realize that creation was in reality a beautiful building process. It is still going on as it strives to build the perfect form, the Body for the Christ Spirit from out of the archetypes of the spirit world.

Now, as the twentieth century has unfolded with its expanded knowledge that the universe is far more than a background for our God's creation of the earth as hinted in Genesis, renowned scientists and astronomers have revealed to us a more realistic theory of how it possibly came about. Even this revelation must stand the test of time. It does infer, however, that there are revelations and theories that seem to explain more clearly, more believable, than the story read to us in Sunday School and at bed-time. These do have a scientific background of deep-space observations and geometric equations.

Another century has just arrived over the horizon. It is time for us to realize that the books we still hold so dear are in reality myths and legends passed down from antiquity to teach us the ancient truths as they were told for the understanding of those early times, to help us form the truths for our day. Man of those ancient days LIVED with nature, with time to meditate on the mysteries of the heavens and the great mystery of his own existence. They, too, pondered, "what guides the stars in their circular path through the heavens? Is our earth affected by them? Where did we come from? What causes all things to happen? Why are we here?" Finally, we are discovering the answers that has eluded man for so long.

Many prophets arose, spiritual men able to reach deep within their intuition and pass these stories down to the tribes as folklore around the campfire, the very beginning of the myths. But even as the parables of Jesus, the last great prophet of Israel, these early myths were truths being unfolded in a way that they could be understood by those who were hungry to know the secrets, but hidden from the uninterested masses.

These were not meant as literal stories for no one was there to see how these things happened. Jesus told many stories that were basically untrue but used the parable as a method of teaching the truths he knew. This is the manner of Eastern conversation, even so far as gross exaggeration. Who counted the people that Jesus fed with the "loaves and fishes" to verify that it was 5000 - or 4000 as in another story?

As the art of writing came forth, these became the history of man's early beginning that we read and study today. The Book of Genesis is just such a book, beautifully telling the legend of the beginning of creation and the formation of the planet called Earth in its time in a manner that those people could understand. But we have allowed this wonderful myth to be so infused in our religion as a literal, truthful, supernatural, six-day creation that we have utterly failed to realize the glorious plan that has been laid before us if we would only grasp its hidden meanings. Even the name, Adam, was mistranslated as a proper name, though, as stated earlier, it was in all probability written to portray mankind, for only then does it and science agree.

This creation was not a failure of God as presumed, wherein He lost His creations to a rebelling underling. Rather, it was the beginning of the manifestation, the revealing in form, of the powers and archetypes that filled the universe. It was the latent energy of Chaos suddenly being turned into kinetic energy of Work, creating these first simple forms from out of its own building blocks within itself.

As the first great outbreath of motion and light took place, so began the revealing of all the archetypes that lay hidden within the Supreme Intelligence, first the simple entities of neurons and protons into the forms we see today. It covers the Spirit's pilgrimage down into matter, from the very first unconscious, undifferentiated states that were formed in the seas to the conscious individualized material being we call mankind.

This will be a new thought to many, and many will no doubt refute it. This is understandable. Our love and feelings for one another should not rest upon agreement. But it will not be heard from a pulpit in the near future, we can be assured of that, for it is not taught in seminaries to be passed to the masses. It does not fit into their fable of The Fall of Man and the great theological redemption now under way which is the very basis of their teachings. But it is proven theories as portrayed by the scientific world which in turn agrees with the age-old wisdom that is now coming forth.

It does not have to be accepted by faith alone. Science has found the key to unlock these mysteries by searching the very depths of the heavens and the rocks and oceans of the earth. It was also revealed to the ancient minds that searched the depths of their intuition through meditative thought and left a trace for us.

This does not mean that future studies will not change somewhat even these concepts, for knowledge is forever expanding and Truth, being nebulous, is also expanding with the abilities of our minds to accept the revealing of the True Deity. What it does, however, is completely cancel the literal story of the man Adam and his help-mate taken from his side. It completely does away with the fall of man through the eating of the fruit of a tree. And without Adam's fall from grace, there was no need for a sacrifice for man's later salvation as we have so wrongfully been told. Instead, we are admonished, ". . .Work out your own salvation with fear and trembling". We must pick up our Cross of Life and follow the pattern that Jesus portrayed in his life. Every thought and action we portray is our responsibility, and must be balanced, either by balancing thoughts and actions or by the reaping of what we sow.

Almost everyone does believe that there was a beginning at some time in the distant past. This has nothing to do with religious belief or the Bible or scientific thought. It seems that man has reached a plateau in understanding when common sense tells him there had to be a beginning for all things of finite form. Both the bible and science states, "In the beginning . ." showing that there possibly was a time when the world of form came from out of the world of spirit. The how and when of that mysterious happening seemingly is the disagreement as we read these stories as told in the myths of every race and tongue.

Most of our theological teaching is that all things were made by "God" from "nothing". The stars were made from "nothing". The earth was made from "nothing", and all things upon it were made from "nothing", except man. He alone was made of the dust of the newly-formed earth. God "willed" in His great mind and all these things came about.

This, of course, is a belief in the absurd supernatural wherein nothing must be proven but the story must be accepted by faith in the story itself. We are told that everything that is passed down through generations and upheld by the clergy must be accepted by faith, for the church world claims infallibility.

That day is fading away. These old myths and legends are being questioned, and well they should be for our very lives depend upon what we accept and believe. Deeper understanding of these age-old stories is coming to light and we must examine them and compare them with the scientific revelations that have come forth in this past century. For science is nothing more than the study by man, himself, and the world around him to open his understanding.

There is really no quarrel between science and religion; religion reveals in parables (in myths and legends) what happened at a previous, unknown time, by a power and intelligence that is beyond man's ability to understand as he still stands in awe and obeisance. Science strives to explain the how by the tracks in the hardened mud and the bones being uncovered after eons of time of being buried and petrified, by the mountains and valleys both above and below the oceans, and the strata pushed up by early volcanoes, signs for us to examine and understand. Some time in the distant past these things were.

As a new century unfolds, more and more people are beginning to question the age-old method of accepting religion as being unquestionable. The day of deeper reasoning is upon us. A spiritual awakening is happening as the dawn of a new day begins to shine. We find that nothing is unquestionable. The mind of Man has developed the ability to reason more accurately so that he can learn and expand. Mysteries still abound all about us, that is a fact that all should recognize, but Mystery is only that which is not understood. It is not supernatural nor magical, but only the universal laws at work in its time and seasons.

Mysteries can turn into truths as we seek for it. But these new thoughts are not to separate us, but rather to broaden our reasoning abilities even more, still leaving us to think and believe as we will in the bond of love and oneness.

Each of us have our own understanding; it is required of us to grow more fully in the light we have and to seek the Path that leads us to a higher plane of existence.

-16-

The Myths of A Faded Past

As we examine the ancient myths and legends of the various races we come to realize that they are in reality only stories of by-gone days, but told to the people in a way so that they could understand their past.

In striving to understand them we find that the story itself is not the mystical message but rather only the container as were the parables of Jesus. The true message must be gleaned from out of these myths themselves, from the symbols they convey and the characters portrayed, and only the seeker will find the truth.

First we must realize that the time for greater revelations is present here in our life-time. Knowledge is increasing faster than most people can absorb it. We can examine so many more things from an empirical viewpoint than was ever possible, and our understanding of knowledge is so much broader. We are finally beginning to use our reasoning to glean the true message out of the fairy-tales of our youth. Surely, we can see that the twenty-first century mind is maturing.

That is what these words are striving to show in as factual a manner as possible. There is no new dogma being brought forth. There is no right or wrong in our beliefs. It is only the ability to understand our beliefs in a new light, for so much has been hidden in the esoteric writings, and the light of theology has been dimmed by its exoteric interpretations and the power struggle for man's mind by the authoritative Church.

Let's take a moment and listen to the ancient words from a myth of our own country, passed down through ceremonies from one great Indian leader to another so the people could understand their origin:

"In the beginning the Great Spirit made the world for His pleasure. He piled up the mountains, scooped out the lakes, traced the rivers, and planted the forests. To dwell in them, He created the insects, the fish, the reptiles, the birds, the beasts, and finally man. Into all He breathed the breath of life which is a measure of the Great Spirit."

All are His children, and man but a little higher than the animals. He is better only in having a larger measure of understanding, and a little better knowledge of the Great Spirit. So also in better gifts. He has the power of hearing the voice from which comes knowledge of the unseen world."

This was referred to as "The Wisdom of the old men." It was added to by another great leader named Walking Buffalo, who said, "We see the Great Spirit's work in everything: the sun, moon, trees, mountains, and the wind. Sometimes we approach Him through these things. For Nature is the book of that great power which one man calls God and another man calls the Great Spirit. But what difference does a name make?"

It is astounding the similarity of the creation of Genesis and these words from another race what we term a savage race. We find a record of the steps taken in this creation, with no indication that all was accomplished supernaturally in one small period of time. Thus, the difference lies in the fact that the Hebrew rendition seemingly added a time table which has been interpreted as a literal time for creation instead of ages.

Even the order of creation is remarkably similar. Only in the creation of man does the similarity end. In our Indian rendition it seems to assume a plurality as if it were mankind, and the fall from "grace" is lacking. Instead, there remains the closeness of man to the Great Spirit throughout time.

The Hebrew rendition speaks of the creation of only one man, Adam and later, his help meet, Eve, formed from out of him. It tells of their unfaithfulness to God and their expulsion from the Garden of Eden. The short history given of them becomes very involved and filled with many unanswered questions.

They bore two children, Cain and Abel. But out of jealousy man's murderous ways began. Cain struck down his brother, Abel, and for this act the Lord sentenced him. "A fugitive and a vagabond shalt thou be in the earth".

"And Cain said unto the Lord, 'My punishment is greater than I can bear. . . .and it shall come to pass, that everyone that findeth me shall slay me'. And Cain went out from the presence of the Lord, and dwelt in the land of Nod, on the east of Eden" (Genesis 4:13,14,16).

"And the Lord set a mark upon Cain, lest any finding him should kill him."

From whence did those come who would find him? From whence came those who lived in the land of Nod that he joined? Whose daughter did he marry to bare Enoch?

We find these old myths and legends are filled with these many questions that the exoteric mind cannot answer. We must seek for the unveiling of them in other places. But it shows us that there was a time called, "In the beginning". It is our duty - to ourselves - to strive to find the true message in each of the stories and blend this into the evolution of the Life-Force from latency to the kinetic manifestation in form.

We are at another crossroads in our beliefs as mankind has reached many times. Such a one is similar to what the Christian world faced in 1514 as Nicholas Copernicus, a Polish priest and church mathematician, produced the heliocentric theory, that the earth and planets revolved around the sun. The Fathers of the Roman Church believed and taught differently, teaching as Aristotle had theorized approximately 300 B.C., that the sun and planets circled the earth and that the earth was the stationary center of the universe.

It took until 1992 for this error to even be acknowledged by the Church. Pope John Paul sought to reconcile science and religion by declaring the error in condemning Copernicus and Galileo as heretics for their theory which since then has been proven undeniably true. This, of course, is only one of the many errors that has come to light in our theology down through time, and the actual issuance of this lone correction has been reluctant and slow.

As we open the bible again to study its writings, we find that it begins with the story of creation told in a different yet very similar manner than the Indian myth. "In the beginning God created the heaven and the earth.

And the earth was without form and void; and darkness was upon the face of the deep. And the Spirit of God moved upon the face of the waters."

Herein lies the first of the confusion as we strive to accept the literal story. The Hebrew word, Elohim, translated as God as a singularity, is a plurality of Eloah but in no sense does it imply the Trinity, the invention of the early Roman Church. It has been interpreted to mean that God "thought" and the material universe suddenly was brought forth. Further study reveals that there was definitely a plurality meant, as we read in Genesis 3:22. "And the Lord God said, Behold, the man is become as one of us, to know good and evil'".

We are told that in the beginning there was nothing but darkness. Suddenly, "The Spirit of God moved upon the face of the waters." We can assume that Movement began, and with it Time began as proclaimed by science. But where did all the water come from? What held it? Nowhere in the writings did it say that God first made the waters and placed them in space before his Spirit moved. What does it really mean? It has never been explained, but rather ignored. We can readily see that it must have been the first of the creative forms.

"And God said, 'Let there be light', and there was light. And God saw the light, that it was good: and God divided the light from the darkness. And God called the light Day, and the darkness He called Night. And the evening and the morning were the first day."

Science tells us that space was nothing but a dark void, empty, non-existent. Upon that point science and religion agree. The age-old writings of Ancient Wisdom termed it the deep sleep or rest between universes of The Father/Mother, a binary, a positive and negative out of which all things are formed, as it strives to explain there was a time before this creation.

179

But there was yet given no Cause for light; the sun was not yet formed. Nor was there an earth to turn to form this first day. This Night and day were formed before the earth could make it possible. In the literal sense, then, we have an Effect before we have a Cause, an impossibility.

But Science explains for us the sudden appearance of light in the darkness of space. It tells that all energy, that of which all forms consist, was compacted around one point. Then came what science has called the Big Bang, the first tremendous nuclear explosion of this hot, compacted energy. With one tremendous flash light filled space. Waves of energy boiled out in great solar winds of the blast and the first primeval substance called Ether was created.

Before that instant there was only latent energy. Then, with one giant explosion Motion and Time began, and Change followed.

"And God said, 'Let there be a firmament in the midst of the waters, and let it divide the waters from the waters.'

And God made the firmament, and divided the waters which were under the firmament from the waters which were above the firmament: and it was so. And God called the firmament Heaven. And the evening and the morning were the second day."

We find again this water, now being separated by the newly-formed firmament called Heaven spoken of as made on the second day. We must assume in our literal interpretation, therefore, that Heaven is a literal place somewhere above us, surrounded by water, and that it was not the eternal home of God and the angels as we have been led to believe but only formed one day before the formation of the earth.

Science tells us that from out of this great explosion of latent energy, through cooling and cohesion, came the neurons and protons which are the most minute building blocks of matter, the particles that form the atoms of the elements. We can surmise, then, that this was the firmament in its earliest stage of formation, and the waters perhaps were the great sea of energy, the aether, in which they floated.

"And God said, 'Let the waters under the heaven be gathered together unto one place, and let the dry land appear:' and it was so. And God called the dry land Earth and the gathering together of the waters called He Seas: and God saw that it was good".

Herein can we vision a point in this great sea of energy, the waters, as selected for a galaxy to be formed, and within it our solar system. This point, this nucleus of energy, was the beginning of our sun, and from out of it came the earth and planets. This was the coming together of the building blocks of matter as the Law of Gravity and Cohesion came into effect.

"And God said, "Let the earth bring forth grass, the herb yielding seed, and the fruit tree yielding fruit after his kind, whose seed is in itself, upon the earth: and it was so."

"And the earth brought forth grass, and herb yielding seed after its kind, and the tree yielding fruit, whose seed was in itself, after its kind: and God saw that it was good. And the evening and the morning were the third day."

Here we find in the literal sense that the earth was made on the third day, 72 hours after the beginning, and immediately, on that day, there came forth the grass, herbs, and trees bearing fruit. Everything was supernaturally formed out of nothing. We do find, however, the first formation of foliage for the needed oxygen before the creation of the air-breathing life forms.

"And God said, 'Let there be lights in the firmament of the heaven to divide the day from the night; and let them be for signs, and for seasons, and for days and years. And let them be for lights in the firmament of the heaven to give light upon the earth.' And it was so."

"And God made two great lights; the greater light to rule the day, and the lesser light to rule the night. And God set them in the firmament of the heaven to give light upon the earth, and to rule over the day and night, and to divide the light from the darkness; and God saw that it was good. And the evening and the morning were the fourth day."

Here we have the creation of the lights to rule the day and the night. We have the sun and moon made on the fourth day. On this fourth day it was stated that the stars that fill the heavens were also made. We have found them to be other suns in our galaxy, though we find them to be billions of years old.

This story, taken literally as it has been taught, would make the sun, the moon, and all of the stars one day younger than the earth which was formed on the third day. This, according to bible genealogy as taught, was only 6000 years ago, though science and Geology have found evidence of a far greater time in examining the tell-tale signs being revealed.

"And God said 'Let the waters bring forth abundantly the moving creature that hath life, and the fowl that may fly above the earth in the open firmament of heaven.'. . . . .And the evening and the morning were the fifth day."

"And God said 'Let the earth bring forth the living creature after his kind, cattle, and the creeping thing, and the beast of the earth after his kind; and it was so. . . And God said, 'Let us make man in our image, after our likeness' . . . . . ."

"So God created man in his own image, in the image of God created He him; male and female created He them . . . . And the evening and the morning were the sixth day."

"Thus the heavens and the earth were finished, and all the host of them. And on the seventh day God ended His work which He had made; and He rested on the seventh day from all His work which He had made."

This, then is the story of Creation as literally believed. But this brings forth a question, a possibility. Could each "day" have been an epoch of time, a period of successive steps in creation, rather than a twenty-four hour period? By whom was the decision made, and by what authority? We find it said, "A day of the Lord is as a thousand years (only a period of time)." If that could be, it would agree with the scientific theory of eras that these episodes happened, and would even coincide with the myth of our Indian story-teller. This would seem a far more logical explanation.

We find, then, that the earth was formed to hold the seas and the life forms that came forth, the trees and the grasses, the fowls of the air, the beasts of the field, and finally man. This is precisely in the same order that the old Indian myth quoted to us, and that science has stated. The time element is the glaring difference. The how and the why that all of this took place has never been theologically explained except that it was supernaturally and out of nothing.

We have been assured by theology that all will be done away with in due time. Has this, then, all been just a waste because of a bite of an apple that looked and tasted so pleasing? Why, then, did it even begin if it depended upon man being loyal? For God should have known the weakness He formed in man by giving him a free will without the experience to guide him.

We find that the literal interpretation depends entirely upon the belief and supposition of an entirely supernatural creation in a natural, six-day time span. It also depends upon the belief of an anthropomorphic God, a SPIRIT BEING doing this by thought. This, of course, is for each individual to believe as they choose, for that is the free-will of man working out his own salvation according to his understanding. That is the inalienable right of us all.

But let us reason together around the mythical campfire, perhaps trading the peace-pipe for a cup of coffee, and see if by chance that science and religion do not contradict one another as presumed, but together they paint a beautiful, believable, and reasonable picture of "In the beginning . . . ".

The "How" of creation is where disagreement begins to separate the knowledge of Science from the faith, belief and superstition of religion. In none of the stories of creation is there a detailed account of how it really came about, so that much of the story had to wait until this Age, until the mind of 20th Century Man could assemble the pieces. By the signs of the lights in the firmament of the heaven (Gen.1:14) as seen through the powerful instruments that has been given man, no doubt for just such a purpose, and the archaeological finds that have been revealed to him, he has formed the details. The spirit within had to show man his origin, but only as he sought it from out of the maze of beliefs.

From out of the ether of outer space he has found that his form was made, and from the bosom of The Absolute did his spirit come, an immortal spark of the life-force that is emitted from out of our sun.

Now the day is dawning when the knowledge of our true self is being revealed to the masses as the age-old wisdom of past avatars comes to

184

light. It is spreading over the earth as the tide comes in to cover the shore, washing it free of the debris of passing days and leaving a foundation of clean, pure sand and rock.

Hidden deep within the ancient manuscripts of lost civilizations has come many revelations of mysteries that Science, Philosophy and Metaphysics are now unveiling for us, so that we might see the Path in a brighter light. This is the Path we all must learn to trod, with the words of Gautama the Buddha and Jesus the Christ pointing the way.

The Way has always been Divine Love and Charity, and the oneness of creation.

-17-

What Does Evolution Mean?

We are finding that the light of Creation is now coming forth to us through the efforts and the inquiring minds, and of course through the efforts of the early astronomers of the 15th century. Sadly, only a few in this age realizes the great step upward that Copernicus, Galileo, and Kepler made for us, and the importance of the continuing search of those of this past century. It has been added to by the philosophers who have filled in many more details as they searched the writings of ancient adepts for hints of possibilities.

We have now finally coming to us in this latter day a new story of creation and the revealing of evolution as written for us in the prophets and philosophers of old and in the stars and the earth itself for us to find.

We speak of evolution here as if it were an accepted fact. Indeed, it has not been accepted by all. To the majority of the theological world it is only a concept, and a very frightening and dangerous concept to be sure. It is surmised to be a direct contradiction of the entire teaching of a supernatural creation some 6000 years ago. This anthropomorphic God, a SPIRIT BEING somewhere in the vastness of the heavens, made all forms complete and perfect, as it has been taught, during this appointed week of creation. Thus, to this group the story of evolution is the fairy tale. But the time has come for the revealing of this concept that has been discovered in the stars themselves.

Evolution has been proven in many ways so that it is an established scientific theory. Slowly and reluctantly it has been accepted by some religionists as shown in 1996 when Pope John Paul II issued his statement that physical evolution is "more than just a theory," a significant step for such as the Catholic Church who has fought against scientific findings for many centuries.

The first thoughts of evolution brings to mind the vision of a large hairy ape as an ancestor. Such a thought is more than our faint little egos can accept and we cast such a theory aside as pure heresy without true examination. But these thoughts are congealed in the minds of people because the theory has never been explained in its fullness and the myths of Genesis has been substituted in our teachings as a literal happening.

Luckily, evolution does not teach the genealogy of the ape family. It does state, however, that all forms originated from one source, from out of the minute particles that began at that moment of "In the beginnings. . This much is agreed upon as a matter of speaking, but the "One Source" seems to be the point of disagreement. So let's examine this question and see if perhaps there can be other points that can be agreed upon instead of only points of argument.

The theory of evolution is the process of development from a rudimentary to a mature or complex state. Simply stated, it is the process of change of all living things from a single molecular state toward the complex forms of the material world of which mankind is the apex - so far. Even more simply stated, it is the continuing manifestation of Consciousness in ever higher realms, from the archetypes of possibilities in the beginning through the many stages and models for the unveiling of itself in its ultimate true form, the Body of the Christ Spirit.

We have shown how the universe began, according to scientific studies. In view of the strata of our earth and the skeletons and fauna that floods and volcanic upheavals have uncovered, we see many thousands and perhaps even millions of years etched before us. We must recognize these things and not turn our eyes and minds away from such facts. Then, with such evidence before us we must weigh it against the interpretations that have come forth of the ancient writings and drawings from all the different races down through time. We must also examine more closely the teachings that we have clung to for so long that really has no evidence for us to study, except, of course, the Jewish bible.

It is rather humorous at times to read in the "Letters to the Editor" column of the newspapers the efforts that many people put forth into their striving to disprove this theory. It seems as if everyone has become endowed with great scientific minds in matters that far exceeds the scope of the ordinary person.

One man has written recently, "There is much evidence to support the Bible. However, faith is the key ingredient for a Christian . . ." There was, of course, none of this "much evidence" given, and faith makes nothing true except to the believer.

"A recent letter in USA Today," he continued, "stated that Christians believe the age of the world is between 6000 and 7000 years. That's ludicrous. We believe the age of man is between 6000 and 7000 years. There is a difference."

Yes, there is a difference. It is three whole days, as depicted in the book of Genesis.

Another Christian wrote, "When I was little and went to church, I was taught that Darwin was a workman of the Devil and that evolution was just some crazy idea that didn't make any sense. When I went to school I was taught that evolution was a fact and that you cannot believe in science without evolution. I have since learned that both of these teachings are not true. When all the evidence of the 'Modern' evolutionary theory are thoroughly examined they don't hold up. There is a major flaw in the way scientists conceive the universe."

Again, we find none of the evidence that has been so "thoroughly examined and found wrong". Neither was the "flaw" identified in the way the universe is wrongly conceived.

After a few more derogatory remarks about evolution, he ended. I wondered what school he had attended that taught evolution. I have heard of none. I looked for the evidence disproving the theory of the universe but found none. He spoke of Einstein's theory of relativity also upsetting the existing order and it, too, was just a mistake in scientific logic. After much thought I felt that I must hold to Einstein's theory just a little longer, until his great mistake is brought more thoroughly to light.

All of these letters I have read are interesting because it indelibly shows the thoughts of many. Seemingly, they have the same thread of thought: the interpretation of the bible is held as the undeniable Truth, without needing any proof. This, of course, is a dangerous assumption. We recognize that it is the unalienable right for everyone to believe in the manner they choose, yet opinions and faith by themselves does not make a sound, believable cause and we should strive to find the truth in all things.

Until one hundred and fifty years ago it was the accepted biological thinking that all species were unchanging down through time and specially made from the very beginning. But questions began arising in the fields of botany and biology as these fields of science grew. From the skeletons and fauna found in the primordial strata it was assumed that these earlier, simpler forms did exist at some time in the far distant past. It was the duty of science, then, to reveal this ancient part of our world to us in a manner that all could willingly accept. So far it has failed to convince the majority as only a few have truly weighed it against the accepted creationism through supernatural methods.

The finding of fossils of extinct species that were SIMILAR to later species brought up a very important question; why did these similar species exist in successive geological periods? They were not the SAME species; only SIMILAR, as if branches of the same tree of life, but in their having to adapt to changing environmental conditions many failed and disappeared. Others changed enough to adapt to the changing environment and survived.

This observation brought up the idea - or theory - that forms in nature could change and adapt over great periods of time according to the needs and the environmental conditions in which they existed. Thus, a new but similar specie evolved.

There is little doubt that Charles Darwin's studies on his 5-year scientific expedition revolutionized the geological and biological worlds.

His was the first new idea in a world of plodding for centuries along the same paths of thinking.

His study of geology showed that sedimentary rock previously covered by water would crystallize by metamorphism when buried by other rock. It changed. Thus were crystals formed. He also studied how volcanoes and earthquakes changed the land masses by uplifting some and sinking others. He theorized the formation of coral reefs by the skeletal remains of dying coral. By these findings and theories, he showed that all things were changing over periods of time to fit the need of the Life Force within.

His greatest achievement came through his biological findings, especially his studies of the array of different species living on different islands off the coast of South America. These islands became his laboratory. Many were related species, but yet differing in some manner.

He found ground finches on each island, but their beaks ranged from small and fine to large and powerful, according to the island on which they were found. He found that these differences were traceable to their eating habits; the large beaked birds ate large seeds accessible on their island, while the small beaked birds ate small seeds and insects in their environment. This, to him, truly showed the adaptability over time of the same species to its environment as need arose.

It was the conclusion, then, to Darwin that certain characteristics that gave a specie a special survival advantage came to be selected over time, and would be passed to the following generations through the changes in the gene structure. It suggested that a CONSCIOUSNESS within each specie needed these changes in characteristics to serve some purpose, and included a brain in the body to control the actions that the consciousness desired, and a reasoning ability that followed later was given to man.

Surprisingly, at nearly the same time and nearly the same part of the world another man named Alfred Wallace was also studying to become a naturalist. Neither knew of the other's studies. But, after years of travel and study their works came together. The theory of evolution through natural selection and the survival of the fittest was summarized in their work and in their writings and showed the trail that the life-force had taken upward through time. Out of it came Darwin's widely read and much criticized book, "The Origin of Species."

The greatest problem, of course, of accepting this new theory came from the sector of religion. This was the foundation of the famous Scopes trial in which the theory of Evolution brought out by Charles Darwin was contested in a court of law against the teachings of the Bible. Darwin's findings and theory were presented with his proofs. Religion had no proof save the bible. Some scientists sided with the religious concept of a God being the perfect Creator, making all things out of nothing. But there were many other scientists who embraced Darwin's theory.

With the trial held in the bible belt of the country it was really no surprise that the jury sided with religion and against the bulk of science and its proofs. They accepted the religious interpretations over Darwin's facts as presented, and that was proof enough at the time that evolution was incorrect. But the jury system was really only the comprehension and opinion of a small chosen group of people, and in no way does it constitute truth in every case as we have found in many trials even in our own time.

Later, added to it but not a part of it was the concept of "The survival of the fittest." Although this idea had its merits, it was a theory that gained little attention at that time and was never examined.

It has been contended that Darwin later retracted his theory. That is untrue. At the age of sixty nine, twelve years after his controversial book, "On the Origin of Species", he wrote another book explaining his idea of evolution from his many years of studying nature throughout the world. It was called, "The descent of Man and Selection in Relation to Sex". In this book he provided the evidence that showed human evolution from more primitive species through the sexual selection of mating.

From then on until his death his life turned to his truly first love, that of Botany. He showed that plants have an inner awareness, a simple consciousness, always turning their growth toward light, and sending tentacles outward feeling for support as they reached upward and outward.

His extraordinary work earned him the distinction of being one of the greatest figures in the field of Biology. If a fault in his work could be found it was because he looked to form and its environment instead of the life-force within that called for the changes needed in its future models.

At his death, he was buried with honors in Westminster Abbey in London, the resting place of the royalty of England. This was not the resting place of a man with outlandish ideas as so many supposed; this was the honored resting place of Charles Darwin, the Father of Biology and a devout believer in evolution.

No discussion of this subject would be complete, however, without examining it in the light of the laws of Thermodynamics. These laws are the ultimate proof of the creationists that evolution cannot be a fact, for there can be no denying the transfer of heat energy from all molecules and systems of matter. These laws state emphatically and undeniably that all bodies must operate at less than 100% efficiency due to the energy expended through friction.

That indeed is a true statement and keeps us from finding the perfect perpetual motion machine. Science tells us that our human bodies operate at only about 80% efficiency, so there is no way that one could deny entropy. We see this all too plainly in our bodies in its span from birth to death and dissolution. This tendency toward disorder is referred to as the "arrow of time" given to all natural forms.

These laws are once again showing the immutable law of change as it continually reacts to the adoption of need. In this natural world of Form, all forms IN EXISTENCE passes from formation through usefulness to disintegration, back into its simpler forms of simple elements as usefulness diminishes.

Evolution as contended defies the laws of entropy. This law, the tendency of all matter to move toward steady and inevitable deterioration, cannot be denied. In the world of form, the Law of Entropy reigns.

With all of this against it, however, evolution still remains a question looking for the plausible explanation. Individual forms do deteriorate. But we do see progression in forms of life over time, leaving room to wonder about that which is within the life-form, the consciousness of individuality. Does the need for greater expression bring forth changes in future generations?

Is death, then, the gateway for the upward progress of the soul as bodies fail because of a need unfilled? The soul must continue it journey upward.

Perhaps an answer can be found in studying it more closely. For through change we see progress, generation after generation.

-18-

Evolution Explained

Let us examine the meaning of evolution once more in this new light. As we have found, many words have changed in meaning through its uses, and many translations often portray only the thoughts that phrases bring to the translator's mind. But these do not necessarily portray the exact meaning of the word nor the thoughts of the writer or speaker being translated, and herein lies the danger.

Evolution is thought to mean, "A gradual process in which forms change into a different and usually more complex or better form". This is not the meaning of evolution. Forms do not change to a better form as agreed just above. After their allotted time forms revert to their original simplest parts, the minerals and gases of which they were made, and the life-force within it withdraws and moves to its original plane, the plane of spirit. This is the Law of Entropy as applied to forms in a closed system into which nothing can be added. It is undeniable, indisputable.

A factor not realized is the fact that the world is not a closed system, but is continually receiving energy from the sun and from other universal sources. It is still evolving to a higher level of existence.

The New Century Dictionary gives the meaning of the word as, "A gradual progress of the universe from simplicity to complexity."

We find, then, the discrepancy in meaning that has never been brought into the discussion of evolution. It is little wonder that it has become such a dissenting factor in our lives, for each side of the argument can well be correct in its stand. Entropy in the world of form is a fact, an immutable law of the universe. But we also discern all about us the gradual progress of forms through time to a more complex design as its environment and use dictates the need. Man's form has been refined to a much higher state through the centuries. Animals have been bred for higher and faster degree of advancement for better uses. It would be a fair statement with these facts to prophesy in another thousand years that man and animal will be evolved even higher, not singularly, but genetically. For some unaccountable reason we do not recognize nor admit these facts as probabilities.

Therein lies the factor of disagreement. The creationists claim that the earth AND its inhabitants have not changed from the very beginning. The evolutionists claim that the earth has changed by its very cooling. It has changed from the steamy, jungle-like atmosphere wherein huge lizard-like birds and animals roamed before mankind. Living entities have changed by the demand of environment, through natural selection by mating, and the survival of the fittest to adjust.

The original meaning of the word in the ancient writings brings evolution to us even in a little different light:

"It is the disclosure or revealing of the highest, most complex realm (The Absolute, The All-Mighty, that which we call God), EXISTING FIRST AS AN ARCHETYPE IN AN UNDEVELOPED STATE OF PURE LATENT UNIVERSAL INTELLIGENCE. By the PROGRESSIVE DESCENT of this original complex archetype of latent energy in its many possible models, down through the different worlds of its manifestation from its perfect state of rest, through its ability to create, it has changed from latent energy into its myriad of MORE SIMPLER FORMS as movement began, for the manifestation of this Intelligence through creativeness for its ultimate use." Now this is very simple indeed to understand, isn't it, once it is explained, simply and accurately!

This was the understanding of the great, renowned mystics of many centuries ago, but as the meaning of words change through interpretations to coincide with beliefs many truths have been lost. It is sad that theology, in its infancy, didn't realize the beauty that the word implies as the Life-force strives upward for manifestation in its myriad of forms, eventually to become the manifestation of the Christ spirit. This Life-force does not die and atrophy. Instead, it is continually reaching upward, from one body to another as it makes the necessary changes for survival.

We see the evidence in the heavens that stars eventually crumble in upon themselves and explode into fragments as their nuclear fuel is spent. Perhaps by now, in this twenty-first century, we should call them suns as they have been recognized. But something has been happening within these suns throughout their eons of time that has been unexplained in the Genesis story. It is the formation of new elements.

Matter has been EVOLVING in these suns from the very beginning through the process of nuclear fusion as we discovered possible in our making of new elements for "The Bomb" of World War II. From the simplest atoms in these first suns, those of hydrogen, was formed into helium through the cooling and the cohesion of particles. Then carbon, oxygen, silicon, etc., eventually forming the atoms of all the elements known to man. Tremendous waves of energy has been thrown off into space, in heat waves, light waves, infra-red waves, gamma waves, and on through the thousands of wave lengths of energy by this still-ongoing nuclear process within the suns, and our earth absorbs and uses this energy to evolve.

Asteroids and comets were first formed out of this debris of gases and elements which in turn, through collisions, formed the planets found throughout space. Thus was our earth formed. Out of the debris of these exploding suns, out of these atoms from space has come the molecules that also formed the amino acids that formed the proteins that built the cells that built the forms in which the life-form eventually could inhabit. This is what has been termed Evolution, a name given to explain this procedure of formation.

Nature as we know it today has come from these first forms, with billions of years in the process. This is the study of astronomy and physics and biology being combined to unveil the details of the beautiful story of Genesis, complete in every minute detail so that man would finally understand his beginnings. We find no contradiction, though interpretations can vary as with all things and, sadly, bring division of minds.

We can see in a few centuries of time that man's body has gone through changes to become a better model, able to do things even more efficiently than the older "models". It is not the same body that has progressed but rather another model that the Ego has needed for its later use. Animals have "progressed", fauna has "evolved" over time. Though entropy overtakes all forms after it reaches a certain age, forcing that particular form or body into oblivion, the generations that have followed have progressed to a better model. The DNA records the changes. What, then, is the explanation of this phenomenon? Let us search for a meaning of this mystery.

As we meditate upon this question the age-old voice of Plato might come again to us. "Know thyself. Presume not God to scan. The proper study is man."

Suddenly, the great light of perception coming from our intuition opens the proper drawer of inner knowledge and we find a clue. The secret of evolution is within ourselves.

We are both finite and infinite. This fact is not noted in the argument against evolution. Our bodies are finite physical forms, answerable to the laws of Nature and entropy; we are accessible to heat and cold, to up and down by the force of gravity, and to birth and death. But we can see how the bodies of people in the tropics have darkened through the ages for survival from the rays of the sun, and the whiteness of the skin to absorb the needed vitamin D from the sun in the higher latitudes. This is only one small example, but one to make us wonder.

The Law of Entropy rules the finite individual forms and in our season our bodies return to the dust of the earth. Apostle Paul assured us that the seed, the body, which we plant does not arise, but a new plant takes its place. Was this a hint of resurrection in a new body? We will examine that further.

The Law of Evolution rules the infinite, the life-force, as it adapts the form of species over time with the changes needed for the environment in which it is placed. What do we really know of the infinite part? It is the true "I" within this body, that spirit from the Absolute, that which some call God and that you and I call "I". We are not the body. We are a particle in the great ocean of Consciousness.

The voice of Jesus whispers to us, "Ye are the sons of God." We suddenly realize that we are SPIRIT and not the nature body.

What has not been recognized is that Man is a triad, body, soul, and spirit. The body is only a vehicle for the life-force within to use for its work. We recognize it as physical matter containing an intelligence (mind), both voluntary and involuntary that knows it is conscious, and within it is its four systems for potential operation; the digestive, circulatory, the respiratory, and the generative systems. Without this inner intelligence it is only matter in its lowest plane of existence, without life and intelligence.

Upon entrance of the intelligence at birth, the body is activated and begins operation through the involuntary nervous system. In time, the sense desires begin working through the nature mind and the body responds to this mind's commands. This is the beginning of the formation of the will, that mind that will control the body throughout its life-time.

As this nature form ages and its usefulness ends the vehicle begins to deteriorate. The consciousness within the form which uses it for its purposes begins to weaken its hold as the conscious mind that controls the vehicle begins to wander, the memory begins to fail, and the drive for further accomplishment weakens.

There comes a feeling as we grow old that we want to shed this old shell and rest. "We want to go Home". Even our gospel songs have echoed this inner desire of our Ego to return from whence it came, to its home. This change in our bodies and mind as the years pass is the factor that is never discussed in the light of usefulness and accomplishments of the Ego, but is that hidden factor that is beginning to be revealed and analyzed. As the body dies and slowly disintegrates, the Ego, the Soul, must leave it and wait for its next habitation.

We have seen the evolution of the automobile as more needs arose. These were fashioned from out of the plane of thought, visualized as form in the imagination of its inventor. So also with all of our inventions; they have evolved into better forms. The originals passed away. New models took their place, but they are still automobiles. Our computers of today are a far cry from the room-filling monsters of earlier times, but they are still computers. So we find that evolution continues on as need arises, from out of the life-force in its need for expression.

Energy cannot be manifested except through form. We cannot see the energy called electricity without the form of the bulb, or its form of motor, or until the flash of lightning. So also magnetism. We cannot see its energy except with a piece of iron with magnetic energy. Kinetic energy is the union of Time and Motion creating "work", and without form there is no work. Without form energy is latent, useless as it was before the beginning of time.

These are the scientific facts we must recognize. These are some of the lessons gleaned from the Schools of Learning through Reason. They are not based on faith or religious belief, nor on what one might presume, but on discoveries made through man's scientific theories as he searched for answers. They have been proven through testing by the scientific procedures of many great minds.

This is nothing more than recognizing the ability and the insatiable desire of the Great Universal Consciousness within us to manifest itself in a form of singular expression filled with feeling, wisdom, sensation and separateness. Each form is a single expression of this inner consciousness, and every atom of this form is permeated with this consciousness of usefulness. Each atom KNOWS its required duty and its place in the form.

Oh, what joy there can be to realize that we are each a free Spirit, a flame, a spark, of the Universal Fire, powerful and wise! That has been the inner dream of man down through the ages of time. To be FREE to manifest the "will of the Father" within us as our intuition pushes us toward creating new worlds and new exiting forms!

That's just what we are! A form containing a spark of the Universal Flame of Life, a son of the Father! We are as leaves on a branch of the Tree of Life, a part of the tree itself. We have not recognized this Guide within us but have instead looked heavenward for guidance. But now we are as Prodigal Sons returning to fulfill the desires of our nature senses while we await our Day of Realization.

-19-

The Rest of the Story

Awakening to a bright new day can be an exhilarating experience for almost everyone. That is what we have before us now as this 21st century opens. We have the promise of a new century, a new millennium, and a new page in our lives waiting to be filled in any manner we choose.

In the same manner, awakening to new thoughts can be equally as exhilarating. Becoming aware of them and the new hopes they can bring us can fill our minds with a feeling of that same exuberance. Surely we can ask ourselves, "Why didn't I realize of that years before?"

We can now feel that we are a part of something bigger than our small daily life. We are a part of our entire solar system. Now we can say "our sun, and our planets." We also are a part of *our* Milky Way galaxy. We are also a part, though rather minute, of *our* great, ever expanding universe. We are no longer enslaved to our bodies as our minds are suddenly free from the bondage of our yesterdays to vision new worlds and new planes of existence. We can fly to our hearts desire on wings of thought.

Or we can, if we choose, dismiss all of these new revelations and continue to breathe the same stale air of finite teachings that have stifled our minds for the last 2000 years with pain and anguish.

Today we can finally realize that the true story of creation has never been told throughout the theological world. It hasn't been taught in our schools because those in charge are steeped in the age-old belief of Creationism, just as it was in the days of Charles Darwin more than a century ago. The Bible belt still exists, though now it encompasses the entire nation, even our government which proudly states, "Under God . . ." But Science has loosened the bondage that has held our minds prisoners for so long and it has opened the age of reasoning, filling our libraries with books on any subject we desire to learn. No longer must we rely upon faith alone to form our beliefs.

We can now begin to understand that our progress in life begins deep in the world of thought as it descends from its latent state of perfect rest down through the spirit worlds of the imagination, visualization and desire to unfold in this physical world of formation. Of the four kingdoms of form, only mankind has reached the apex of imagination and the ability to reason. The Elohim, the hierarchies of creation, truly realized that, "Man has become as one of us. . .", for man has become a creator through the power of thought.

We are finding that evolution is not the story of the ancestry of primates as so many fear, nor are we from the bosom of Adam, the nature body. It is the revelation coming forth that we are from the Great ocean of Creative Spirit, and that it forms the vehicle needed for its own attainment.

Jesus stated quite emphatically, "Before Abraham was, I am". We, too, can repeat that same statement. Death is not the end for us, but only a change of attire for the soul, so that it can continue its upward trend toward fulfillment.

The realm of all possibilities and archetypes were in the Universal Consciousness from the beginning, just as the statue is in the block of marble before the chisel strikes its first blow. As motion and time joined to create "work" there began the unveiling of the Universal Mind in form as model after model of all the different bodies were made. First came their initial stages of simplicity in atoms, then combining into molecules, and finally into the simple forms of life. From thence has come the more complex forms of usefulness as we can see in our world of form today. Into the very atoms of each form was the essence of the Universal Mind placed as an intuitive guide, for every atom knows its place and its use in the form wherein it is assigned.

From that instant of time this great Intelligence that is the nucleus of every atom has ceaselessly struggled upward, striving to attain a body of usefulness, building and discarding its many models as it reached upward toward its ultimate. And, as the lifeforce, the consciousness of being conscious, evolved through these steps upward through the four kingdoms of the physical world, so also did the forms evolve as needed. For what it needed it supplied out of itself and discarded the unsuitable.

We see, then, from that first instant of time that we call "in the beginning", it was only the Almighty Absolute Mind in that thick block of marble awaiting for the chisel of energy and motion to unveil it. At first it was the binary Father/Mother, the positive and negative of creation and life, the great super soul of vibrant energy. For want of a name which we must have as we strive to understand, our forefathers named it "The Great Spirit". Later, as man began forming his religions, some began calling it "Elohim", "Jehovah" and finally "God", giving it a Spirit form and a conscious mind and emotions as our own, able to talk and to feel. It became an anthropomorphic God of form, made of a substance as stated in the Nicean Code, and man began worshipping it. Thus we can write, "In the image of man did man create God."

Now, in this new day new revelations have come forth, and we find this Absolute is as an ocean of living energy throughout space. We, as entities, are as minute droplets, minute monads, that are scattered, singularily, over the waters. Each entity is a part of this great ocean of Universal Mind we call aether, but none are the ocean itself. It takes all the droplets to make an ocean.

This is the mystery that is being unveiled in these later days. In the deep studies of the first building blocks of matter by science and psychology, we are finding it wrapped within itself before it all began. Then, as the age-old legends tell us, "The great Mother breathed outward and creation was born." In a burst of brilliant light the Imaginative Thought began breathing forth all the archetypes-to-be in the suddenly expanding universe. "The Spirit of God moved upon the face of the waters."

First came the Son, the Word or movement from out of the Great Mother. "Through Him (motion) were all things made.." From out of the Word came the Hierarchies (Elohim), the Builders and the Spirits, the waves of energy, as Helpers in their descending order. Down through the worlds of formation they came, from the world of Spirit (energy) to the first formative world of Existance or Possibilities, through the worlds of Thought, through the Will to Do, through the world of Desire to the physical world of Formation. This, we are beginning to surmise, is the pattern of the Divine Plan of the Ages for the manifestation of Energy.

This, surprisingly, is the exact pattern that the gurus of today teach in their schools and books as the secret of success. First comes the imagining seed as we vision our goals. This is followed by the visualization of the mind, the formation of the archetype of that to come. Then comes the desire for the fulfillment of the possibilities. But only until *ACTION* begins (motion and time equals "work") can the desire become the form of reality. It takes action in the form of controlled movement for the vision to become a reality.

At long last modern man is discovering the mystery of creation that was known long ago by the mystics, but hidden in their religions for only the seekers to find. He has used his religions to build his carnal societies in all their glories - and all their failings. It has created a divided world instead of a world of oneness and Charity.

But now we are finding the pattern; from out of the Absolute, the Father/Mother of creativeness, the binary Positive/Negative waves of energy, has come the Living Entities in their many forms and stages of intelligence, with man being the pinnacle of the singular intelligence in form. Great avatars and saints have been sent to teach the Living Entities in the many races, and each avatar and saint given the needed wisdon for that time and that race. We of today are of those Living Entities, to learn the lesson of Life and Creation through experiences and intuition.

We can now begin to understand that "evolution" is in reality the striving for the unveiling of the Universal Intelligence in form. From latent complex energy in the beginning it has become individualized kinetic energy, the energy of time and motion combining into matter for the ultimate accomplishment of its duties. It has become Living Light in form, similar to electricity in our homes becoming light through the wires and bulbs, its way of manifestation. It is the life force "that lighteth every man that cometh into the world." It cannot be destroyed by death, but can be changed as the need arises for its continued upward climb through form.

What are we really talking about when we speak of the Father, the Son, the Spirits and Angels and such? These are word symbols of man's attempt to understand the forms of this great Intelligence, that of vibratory waves of energy. Sound, light, x-rays and gamma rays, through the entire spectrum of millions of wavelengths, all forms of matter are really nothing more than waves of energy at different levels. Even at the minute center of the particles that form the atoms we find nothing more than energy whirling around a central point - by cohesion. But nowhere in the universe has the God of religion and His Heaven ever been found.

Thoughts are also waves of energy that we send out into space. We don't realize that these thoughts have energized centers themselves, cohering with other similar thoughts of the same wave lengths to create a phenomenon called mass ideas. It can be a higher force or it can become a seething mob force or even anarchy if not controlled.

Thus do we have cause and effect through our thoughts; whether it is a good effect of joy as in a gala affair or a bad affect of mob violence depends upon the character. But, "where two or more gather in my name, there will I be." Whether it be for good or evil depends upon us.

How often has each of us suddenly had a great thought or inspiration come to us "from out of the blue"? Perhaps we should wonder from whence it came, to be delivered to us. But this is our intuition striving to guide us, in tune with other intuitions in other people.

Now we can begin to understand some of the words of Isaiah. For instance, as speaking for God, he said, "I form the light, and I create darkness. I make peace and I create evil. I the Lord do all these things." (Isaiah 45:7)

"Behold, I have created the smith that bloweth the coals in the fire, and that bringeth forth an instrument for his work; and I have created the waster to destroy." (Isaiah54:16)

There is no other source - for good or bad - save the "I AM ALL!"

Theology, however, has given us a Satan - from out of the belief of Zoroasterism from out of Chaldea, to blame for all the evil. Yet we find Satan and God together, dickering over Job. Did they, too, dicker in the Garden over Adam?

It is time for us to believe in only one Creator, for Good and Evil are only the positive and negative forces striving to bring harmony and balance to the universe. The suns throughout space give off waves of energy that bombard us continually. Our own sun is the very source of life and energy through its millions of vibratory waves. It can also be a killer under certain conditions. Man has created confusion in his mind by giving names for different levels of energy waves without trying to understand these great mysteries. We still cannot define what energy really is except to give it symbols such as God, Jehovah, Allah, or Krishna, names given to the deity in the different languages and religions. We have names such as electricity, magnetism, and gravity in the scientific world, showing that both types of names are used for the same entity. Again we find that science and religion meet on the same level.

Now we come to the question that no doubt has entered many minds. "Does understanding the Big Bang theory of creation and all that it entails really mean anything to us? Will believing it change a thing in our normal way of life?"

Our answer, then, without hesitation should be a resounding "Yes it will!"

We can already see where believing the religious concept has led us directly toward wars of hatred between one another. It has divided us into a thousand different beliefs, each thinking that it has the Truth. It has created individualism instead of a society for all. It certainly has not led us towrd a society of brotherly love as was depicted at its beginning.

If we understand that each of us is a spark of the Universal Intelligence striving to unfold the latent powers of creation within us as we are instructed by our intuition, then we can realize true evolution and true spiritual growth.

Our knowledge is continually changing and increasing. Here in this new day we should strive to understand more through meditation as Jesus showed us in his "mountain" sojourns, We must continue to grow while living in this world of illusions if we expect to find the pearl of great price. We must weigh all things and ideas, what is shown by geology, anthropology, psychology, cosmology, and many other ideas, and not be blinded by pride and predudice. Truth is not swayed by faith or by belief or by sincerely. Truth must stand the test of time and proof.

The decisive question that faces us is, "Are we really a spirit entity in a finite body and world? Are we a part of the Infinite Consciousness? Are we Mind instead of Body?" If this is a possibility, then our vision should turn from the futile, finite life we live today and strive toward building a better, infinite world of brotherly love, for we are all relatives in the same great family.

In the world of science that is a part of our world that tries to find truth behind all things and happenings, the Big Bang theory is far more than just a plausible theory. There will always be new ideas, changes, and ramifications to all ideas as time reveals more of the great mystery of the universe. But for now it is beginning to answer the questions of our ancient past in a far clearer light, and in turn is opening up questions that have been evaded down through time. Why are we here? How did it happen? Why is there such a differnenc in birthrights? Is there a meaning to life?

Without these questions being answered, there is truly no way of knowing about the possibilities of a future and the importance of our daily living habits. It is far better to know these things than trying to hold onto myths by faith alone and never trying to understand the message they contain.

The future will always bring truths and surprises. But let us not return to the days of thinking that the earth was flat and the the sun and planets circled it. Let us not think that the earth is the center of the universe Though these were a truth centuries ago. We simply cannot be God's greatest and only creation of life in a universe of such grandeur and vastness, and have fallen out of His favor so easily, by one small mistake. If so, God has failed miserably in His creative abilities.

Times have been changing rapidly, The twenty-first century has arrived. We have wasted so many lifetimes because of our lack of ability to understand the laws of the universe. We have wasted so many lifetimes because of our ignorance and prejudices. It is time that we began reaching out to one another and reaching for the new horizons that we feel are possible for us.

Out of the great orderly plan of Spiritual Evolution, people are called out of the church world to seek deeper meaning in the world of Metaphysics and the world of the occult. To the unininitiated these are the worlds of belief in magical powers, though they are in reality only spiritual studies of the mysteries of life.

This is the DAY when the milk of spiritual teaching that pervades the denominational sects no longer satisfy the longings for deeper understanding. The individual begins searching for the meat spoken of by Paul, and the teachings that were taught verbally by Jesus. As the mind opens and the heart desires those deeper truths, the esoteric world of greater understanding begins to open. "Seek and you shall find" becomes a reality. The scriptures become alive with a new and beautiful meaning, far from the cruelty of the Law, and the person begins to hear the Voice from within.

Spirit has always been knocking at the door of our intuition, but if our minds are closed to that which is not doctrine -Church delivered - the door will not open.

The history of Christianity is the story of the Passion, a suffering Christ who gave His life to the Father for the sin of Adam. It is the religion of a suffering Love, the story of One who gave His life so that all who would accept the story would be rewarded. It is the religion of agony and tears. By faith in this philosophy that we have been redeemed by His death gives us the feeling of being "Saved",

But also being responsible for his death by being born into sin.

But At-one-ment with the Father is through wisdom and charity, not through blood and suffering.

-20-

The Law of Karma

Everything within the vastness of the universe has been guided by immutable laws according to the purpose and plan from the beginning of time. Our sun with its solar system of planets moves in its appointed path around the center of the Milky Way of which we are a part. It does not move helter-skelter throughout the many arms of the galaxy filled with other suns. The moon also stays in its circular path around the earth. Comets whiz by us in their appointed paths as well, though sometimes the paths of these heavenly bodies intersect at a precise moment and collisions occur. But if it were not for these laws and chosen paths chaos would rule the heavens.

The Law of Attraction of protons and electrons has created the atoms of the elements. The law of cohesion has formed these atoms into molecules and holds them together to create the forms of matter. The Law of Gravity holds these forms of nature to the earth.

All about us we can see these signs of control that govern the physical world we call nature. Many other laws have been discovered within the past century to help us understand some of the mysteries, but many mysteries still remain.

These laws have unfolded as our search of knowledge of the universe has expanded, showing us the rhythmic balancing that continually goes on all about us. We may think of it as destiny or the Will of God, but in reality it is the over-all Law of Balance that must be attained or chaos would reign over space and all of creation therein.

There is also a law even in this School of Drama we call Living. This is this universal Law of Cause and effect. "For every cause there is an effect". In the Eastern world where it was conceived it is referred to as the Law of Karma, in which our actions and thoughts are the causes that writes our potential destiny. It states very emphatically, "Whatsoever a man soweth, that SHALL he also reap." It was also referred to by Jesus in His teachings of sowing and reaping of good and bad seeds.

We ignore it in the striving to fulfill our own desires in our own little worlds, never realizing the suffering or joy that the sowing brings us and others in its effects. But it decrees that our daily decisions must have their own consequences in fulfillment.

Our religions, however, have created a source of our difficulties outside ourselves in the form of a Devil. "He made me do it". It also offers us forgiveness of our actions by our deity without any method of canceling the effect that might have harmed another. We find, then, in our beliefs no true responsibility of our actions or the effect they might have had even upon another through repentance even though the effect can never be reversed. There is no balance in this manner.

For every effect there must be a cause. There is no vengeance of a Deity. There is no judgment. But just as the law of gravity states, "What goes up must come down", so does the Law of Karma state that a thrown stone will strike some target before it stops. Jesus stated that even a lustful thought contained in the action itself is lust. So we see that Karma is the record of the thoughts *and* actions that each of us incur in our lifetime, both the cause and the effect.

This does away with belief that Chance is the ruling power of our lives. This tells us also why we suffer or are rewarded in our lifetime. The Law of Chance is only the belief of the avid gambler who believes that he can beat the odds and win.

Karma is an impersonal law. Our bible teaches us that "It rains upon the Godly and the ungodly." It cannot be swayed nor can it be canceled by prayers, for the Cause has been enacted and Effect invariably follows in its time. This law will be obeyed, and the suffering we feel and see all about us is the balancing that must take place.

This great hidden Law was also realized by the ancient mystics and was taught both by Guatama the Buddha and by Jesus the Christ. It is once again coming forth, this time to the western world after being buried for so long by the Medieval Church. We have been "protected" for so long by our religion that we never realized that there were reasons for these things happening to us, and that we were continually forming our future by our very actions. But even through those dark and trying times there was always the mysterious Alchemy practices, the symbolic Tarot cards, the hidden teachings of the Grand Order of Freemasonry and the Rosicrucian Order to continue the seed of knowledge onward and upward.

The Reformation era of the 15th and 16th centuries brought the realization that there were these physical laws that had to be obeyed. This turned the belief in religious experiences induced by symbols and rituals of the Church to the more realistic thought that empiricism and inductive reasoning were more reliable sources of knowledge than faith alone. Thus began our scientific studies of the world and the resultant reliance on the ultimate laws could be seen as an answer.

We find, then, the mystery behind "An eye for an eye" of the old Mosaic Law, so wrongfully interpreted by the leaders of the Israelites. To them it was the right to seek their own revenge against their enemies. This warring nomadic race failed to understand the true Law of Life and accepted that which we read in the seventh chapter of Deuteronomy as the fulfillment of the Promise given to Abraham.

Please read this chapter to understand the God of the Israelites. It was not the loving, creative Father of which Jesus taught. This jealous, vengeful "Jehovah" allowed them the slaughter and the slavery of their enemies, never realizing that it was the homeland of those whom they conquered. They believed that they were God's chosen people above all others, such as we have today in the Christian belief, and the land in which they confiscated was their Land of the "Promise". But the Law of Karma has made this nation of Israel pay dearly for its abuses of others as it refused to heed the warnings of its prophets.

This Law of the universe is not vengeful as it seemingly is taught of the sayings of Paul in Romans 12:19. ". . .For it is written, 'Vengeance is mine'; I will repay', saith the Lord". This would call for a spirit BEING continually watching over us as our protector and accuser, punishing those who trespass against us. As we read this quoted scripture from Deuteronomy 32:35, we can easily understand the difference.

"To me belongeth vengeance and recompense; their foot shall slide in due time. For the day of their calamity is at hand, and the things that shall come upon them make haste." All will reap what they sow, both good and bad.

Therefore, avenge not ourselves which would create nothing but harmful Karma for us. We need not judge. We need not fear, for, "Their foot shall slide in due time." The Law of Cause and Effect, the Universal Law of Balance will justly rule even as the Law of gravity rules.

The universe is constantly striving for balance as the pendulum swings to and fro with the action of cause and effect. In the East It is called the Great Wheel of Life. The Cause is at the top of the wheel. This tells us that our suffering is of our own making as we allow our desires to influence our innermost thoughts and actions. If this great Law is correctly understood by persons of some intelligence it would no doubt be more of a deterrent because responsibility for our destiny would then be realized to be ours alone.

But does this sowing and reaping all happen in one lifetime? We do not find this to be so. People are born with defects and under terrible living conditions before any cause could possibly have happened. Others seemingly live a life of ease but their present actions harm many. Where, then, is the balancing of the Law?

Jesus explained this about the man who was blind from birth in John 9:1-3. His disciples asked if the man had sinned or did his parents, to bring on this blindness. Jesus replied that neither the man nor his parents had sinned, but it was "so that the works of God could be made manifest". It was the Law of Cause and effect at work. The effect of the Karma from a previous life that had not been paid was being balanced in this new life, with the same ego that was responsible, though now in a new body.

It is taught, however, that it was to show God's great healing power through Jesus. But let us not forget that millions of people who have been born blind without this healing power available. It is indeed a very lame reasoning.

We know that the body dies and returns to its earthly atoms. The ego, the "I" or soul does not die, but returns to its spirit body to await its next incarnation, still responsible for its unpaid Karma. We know, also, that the body only does as the mind wills it to do. It is only a vessel for the Ego to use in its fulfillment of our desires. We can then reason that the "body" itself does not sin nor is at the root of cause. But our will is allowed to be led by the senses instead of being led by the intuition, or by the inner mind. Our own lusts and desires, then, are our own tempter. I cannot blame my unmerciful faults on a mythical Devil someone conjured up. I will reap what I sow, just as everyone will, regardless of death of the body.

what then, when the body dies, if there are many causes or actions that have not been paid? Does death-bed repentance erase all? We find the belief in Purgatory as a place for the soul to go after the body dies, a place of purification for those repentant of their sins. But can a cause be erased after it has happened? Where, in this belief, is the reaping of that which has been sown? There is no balance achieved unless there is an effect. An effect cannot be erased through repentance, a sorrowful feeling. This does not agree with their bible's teachings of the payment of every farthing due. It also does not explain why one is born with the infirmities and another healthy. Let's examine this further.

Throughout the teachings of the ancient mystics we find the thought that the soul, or psyche, is immortal, a drop from the ocean of Universal Consciousness, and always returning "home" to the ocean. It is as a drop of water that always remains a drop of water no matter how many times it is raised to water the earth. It is that which has been given a body of atoms and molecules for evolving to a spiritual entity, though able through its own mind and free will to manifest Good or Evil with its body, whichever it chooses. Its purpose, though not known, is striving to return "Home", never having to leave again to the school of form. This brings the question, "how many people realize or has heard of such a fact? With this thought we can begin to realize that, just perhaps, that this spirit soul will return in another body to act once again in this drama of life, hopefully to right the wrongs its Ego has done, and to learn its part more perfectly, so that eventually it can become a Christ such as Jesus.

We are taught that a new soul is made at every birth, which means that thousands are made each moment. Of what are they made? Where did they come from? Is this just another supernatural act that doesn't need explaining? This would mean that there are already trillions of souls awaiting Judgment Day, with thousands being added each moment, and all with karma that had never been paid.

Surely there would need be a pattern for each soul, whereby all would be born in equal circumstances to be judged equally. We find, however, a great discrepancy in the gifts and birthrights that each is given. We are not as copies of even our parents, though similarities in body do exist through our DNA. Are we then to believe that souls are arbitrarily turned out in these vast numbers and only by the luck of the draw do we receive our parents and our heritage? Questions abound, but they are never answered.

We look upon ourselves as being the body. This body, however, is a nature body made from a nature seed of the elements of this earth. Within it are units of the senses that function as transmitters of impressions to the nature mind within its brain, the Ego. These in turn are given to the will, to weigh through reasoning and intuition, to then command the body to act in a certain manner.

There is, however, a consciousness within this body that is conscious of being "I". Even though the body might be paralyzed, this "I" is still conscious. Even though the body is asleep, this conscious "I" can travel the world and realize many things. This consciousness is the soul, at times called the psyche. This is a spark of life-force, a unit of energy from the One Almighty Consciousness that pervades all space. We find, then, there are two distinct minds that we never realized existed before, the Doer or carnal nature-mind which controls the nature body, and the Thinker, the reasoning mind. But there is still another mind which has never been acknowledged. It is the Knower mind. This is the Father within that Jesus spoke of, the True Self.

Now we have the Triune Self, Body, the Mind, and the Spirit. Only the Doer, the carnal mind, is embodied in and a part of the nature body itself, and is moved and mainly controlled by the senses. The Knower and Thinker are not "in" the body as a part of it, but rather permeates it as a presence. They are as guides only, not as controlling entities of the will, but striving to correctly guide us through our intuition.

The soul is an immortal entity, that spark of the Universal Intelligence that we call God. "Before Abraham was (the nature body), I am." Each of us can state that as a fact of life. The body "dies", disintegrating into its material elements at death. The soul is spirit that comes into the body at birth and exists in a higher world of thought and spirit.

"Never was there a time when I did not exist, nor you, nor all the kings; nor in the future shall any of us cease to be. As the embodied soul continually passes, in this body, from boyhood to youth and then to old age, the soul similarly passes into another body at death."

Here we find a clue in the ancient writings of the Bhagavad Gita of Aryan India of the possible nature of the soul and the body. "The self-realized soul is not bewildered by such change. That which pervades the entire body is indestructible. No one is able to destroy the imperishable soul. Only the material body of the indestructible, immeasurable and eternal living entity is subject to destruction."

You may ask, "Where in the bible can we find such a teaching?" Let us look once again at John 9:13 in this new light. It was so that the works of God could be made manifest. It was the Law of Cause and effect at work which was not canceled even by the man's previous death.

The Plan or work of God is plainly shown to those who would study and accept the possibilities. The effect of the Karma from a previous life that had not been paid was being balanced in this new life.

We are taught, instead, that he was blinded so that the powers of Jesus could be made manifest. Is not this a very inhuman way to display a talent that only a few people might see? It is rather an attempt to grasp at straws for interpretations of things we don't understand. What of all others born blind since that day? If we examine it in the light of the Law of Cause and effect we can begin to absorb the true meaning and find the justification that it should have.

Does this sowing and reaping, then, all happen in one short life- time? People are still being born with defects and under terrible living conditions before any cause could have happened. Others seemingly are born to a life of ease. Where, then, is the balancing of this law, unless we revert to the gambling game of Chance?

We know that the body dies and returns to its earthly atoms. We also know that the body's actions are as the mind wills it. It is not the body that sins, and it dies because of its inability to perform its duties ay further. It is the lust of the senses through the desires of the mind and the will that is the root of all causes. The will has been given the freedom to be led in the direction of its own choosing; we must be careful which god we choose to follow. Our own lusts are the tempter within us.

I find, then, that I cannot blame my unlawful, unmerciful faults on a mythical Devil someone has conjures up. I will reap what I sow, just as everyone else will do. I must be responsible for my thoughts and actions for I will repay every farthing.

This is also the grace of God, giving us the opportunity to learn and balance everything so that we can evolve to be Christ-like, full of love wisdom. The great Play of Life does not end at the drop of the curtain of death, for there are many acts to follow until the play reaches its happy climax and ends with the return of the Prodigal Son to his Father.

Herein we find how Karma and Rebirth come together to form the pathway for the soul. This Divine Plan of the Ages is now beginning to be unfolded before our very eyes. It is for each of us to be "reborn", (changed in the twinkling of an eye) even in this life so that we will have no more coming and going through the doorways of birth and death.

-21-

The Beautiful Law of Grace

Now we come to the realization of the meaning behind the parable of the Prodigal Son. It is a beautiful story, showing the deepest love for a son - or daughter - that man could ever show. Nowhere in it was ever shown bitterness of the Father toward the drifting son as he seemingly squandered his life and fortune. He waited patiently for signs of remorse and regret in the son, seemingly knowing that the time would come when the prodigal would return.

The day did come, just as the father knew in his heart it would. It was a joyous celebration, though the older, faithful and pious son, felt betrayed. But the father explained that the older son was always with him, and still retained his inheritance, and the party was for the return of the one who had been considered dead.

Nowhere in this beautiful story was there a hint of blame, of remorse toward the prodigal son. Nor was there a hint that the killing of the fatted calf was an act of forgiveness, for no forgiveness was needed. The sons, both of them, were always sons.

As we study deeper into the mysteries of life We find there are laws in effect that we must obey or we shall not dine at the Master's table. By disobeying these laws we separate ourselves from the Father and not have been cast out. It has been completely ignored in the religions of the western world, though it was taught by Jesus and Apostle Paul.

In Galatians 6:7 Paul warns, "Be not deceived, God is not mocked. For whatsoever a man soweth, that shall he also reap." It is the Law of Cause and Effect that we have spoken earlier. It is a part of the Divine Plan of evolution.

Herein lies the mystery behind "An eye for an eye". Herein is an explanation of "Whatsoever a man soweth, that shall he also reap". Within these statements as they are written came the belief in a vengeful God who will destroy in an eternal fire those who disobey Him. But wherein then, we might wonder, can we find the beautiful law of Grace and forgiveness in such a deity?

The mystery is now being revealed in its true beauty. It is the revelation that coincides with the patient, loving Father awaiting the expected return of His prodigal son. We find no condemnation in the heart of this Father as He waits for His son to realize the folly of following his own desires and return home. The son must learn the lesson of life just as we, and suffer the pitfalls that he builds just as we ourselves must do.

Throughout the universe suns have formed and suns have exploded in death, and "God" has looked on. Galaxies have collided and "God" has allowed it to happen. The tiny sparrow has fallen to its death, and "God" has watched it fall. The rain falls on the Godly and on the Ungodly in the same manner. Man still goes through his allotted time praying for guidance and relief from the calamities that befall him, and "God" still looks on.

Wherein, then, is the grace and the protective hand of "God" that we cry out for? We cannot understand nor explain this. We say that it is God's will. We were assured in these same writings, however, that if we asked we WOULD RECEIVE. This is a part of the mystery that is unexplained.

We realize now that through the Grace of God everything is balanced. Our thoughts and actions of today bring forth their effects in their allotted time. It is not always instantaneous. It may take years; it might even take lifetimes. But God is not mocked. For every cause or action there is an effect; for every effect there is a cause. If one plants good seed he will in its time reap a good harvest. If one plants bad seed, or tares and thistles, he will reap a disappointing harvest. There is nothing that could be more fair.

In Deuteronomy 32;35 IT IS WRITTEN, :To me belonged vengeance and recompense; Their foot shall slide in due time." Balance must be attained. Patiently, the Universal Mind waits for us to "work out our own salvation with fear and trembling" (Philippians 2:12) as the pendulum swings back and forth in perfect balance.

There have been many conclusions drawn of this Grace of God that is preached. Nearly all of them depends upon a spirit BEING, a God of human attributes awaiting our every move. Supposedly, our every act and thought is recorded in our Book of Life by our Guiding Angel, to be brought before us on the Day of Judgment. We are taught that the blood of Jesus was shed for the sin of Adam, to erase its curse from us. But as we understand that creation and Adam were only an analogy to show in a minute way the beginning of time, we understand it in a far different light.

Raymond Moyer

Let us examine it in a new light. There is little history of the young years of Jesus, except percepts we have of them, and his sojourns "up the mountains", in reality his stealing away in solitude for meditation. His choice of a spiritual life could easily be his "death", his old self buried by baptism by John the Baptist. He rose from out of this watery grave a new man, the example and the way of salvation for all.

But can we be forgiven our deeds through prayer? This was one of the theses that was condemned by Martin Luther regarding teachings of the Roman Church of which he was a part. We can confess our "sins", one to another, as Jesus taught, but there can be no reversing an effect caused by our deeds. The effect of these deeds can never be erased, for someone could have already suffered, or something destroyed. We are judged, so it is taught, each by the same yardstick without measuring the level of each person. There must be a balance even in judgment in some measure that is not understood. It is up to us to remain blameless which perhaps could postpone or soften the Karma.

In the sixteenth century Martin Luther wrote, "We are saved by grace and not by works". His was the message that salvation could not be attained by good works but only through accepting the sacrifice of the Son. This led to the many branches of the Protestant movement down through time with this attitude that good works was not needed for salvation. It could come only through the Grace of God, through faith in the death of Jesus for forgiveness.

Much earlier, in the first century, Apostle Paul taught of the importance of faith. Jesus taught, "Thy faith has made thee whole," showing faith, or confidence, is needed. But faith alone is empty. In the book of James, chapter 2, we find the importance of works. Let us read for a moment.

228

"What does it profit, my brethren, though a man say he has faith, and has not works? Can faith save him? If a brother or sister be naked and destitute of daily food, and one of you say unto them. 'depart in peace, be ye warmed and filled; notwithstanding you gave them not those things which are needful to the body; what does it profit? Even so faith, if it has not works, is dead, being alone." (James 2:14-17).

Martin Luther was an Augustine Monk trained in the Catholic Church with a doctorate of Theology. His indignation was aroused over many of the doctrines being taught. One of the greatest of the practices he abhorred was the Doctrine of Indulgences, the payment of money for the remission of temporal punishment for sins committed after acceptance of Christ but confessed to a priest for forgiveness.

One sale, in 1517, was sponsored for the appointment of Albert of Brandenburg to Archbishop of Mainz. All of the diocese in his jurisdiction brought in enough money through the sale of these Indulgences for the construction of St. Peter's church in Rome. To Luther these "sales" for forgiveness were absolutely an ungodly act for the Church. On October 31, 1517 he posted his famous 95 theses on the church door in protest, and this practice being one of them.

He taught that by Grace God forgave man for the Fall of Adam, if only man would accept it "by faith." Although Luther was correct in his assumption according to the Christian belief of salvation, and James was also correct in that one was still responsible to obey God's command of works as he continued, "Was not Abraham our father justified by works, when he offered Isaac his son upon the alter?" (James 2:21). it is the interpretation of this Grace that creates the problem between illusion and truth.

In the teachings that have been passed down to us we find that Atonement has been a belief by faith more than a way of life to be followed. This became a great problem with the Jewish religion in the days of the prophets as they cried out to Israel to abandon their ways and return to Godliness. We now find ourselves far into the age of reason whereby our minds should be examining the old ways for the messages contained therein and making the changes necessary in our lives to bring forth this new age. It takes faith in our vision, but it must be built on the foundation of works.

For centuries the true message of Jesus through Paul and his followers was threatened by extinction by the medieval church as it preached only the message of the Cross as taught by Simon Peter. Only through devious ways, through alchemy and tarot cards, through the hidden teachings of the Rosicrucians and Freemasonry, and through word of mouth from teacher to initiate did this Gnostic teaching manage to survive. But the cost was high in precious lives as the brand of heretic placed upon them brought death to those who taught and to those who listened.

The type of grace that has been taught first accuses us of guilt. We are guilty of being born into the family of the mythical Adam. This grace is offered to us, but with its stipulation that we must accept it completely by faith. Without this acceptance there can be no salvation, regardless of our good works. The Law of Karma is never mentioned.

There must be this guilt before there can be the need for this saving grace. But even the innocent creatures are suffering from this "sin of Adam", and, sadly, there is no plan mentioned for their salvation. By being and acting as free-will humans we are condemned, though we walk in the light that we have been given. We are born in sin through heredity by the first use of free-will by Adam, but we have not been trained to act any differently.

Accusation of guilt demands an accuser and the necessity of restitution. We must also realize that accusation demands an accuser with a mind capable of thinking and reasoning such as man possesses. This, then, demands God, our accuser, to be a BEING, be it material or spiritual. This is the anthropomorphic God, the God of Christianity and the God of Grace of which they preach to their flocks. It is offered not freely as was His sentencing of us, but rather with the stipulation that it had to be accepted entirely by faith, a theory without proof.

The word ATONEMENT was construed to mean the reconciliation of man to the Father by the death of Jesus. This supposedly was God's plan of salvation for man according to Christianity. It requires the belief by faith that Adam had "fallen from Grace" and thrust from the Garden, and that the Son had given Himself as a sacrifice to the Father for man's deliverance. Sadly, this fallacy has continued even unto this day without questioning. What father would sacrifice one son to death because another son ate a portion of a forbidden apple? Somewhere, some time, the analogy seems to have been misinterpreted.

The archaic meaning of the word ATONEMENT, originally written as At-One-Ment, is "to set at one", with the meaning of coming together, reunion. Each of us must ask ourselves, "Was there a literal "fall of man" as we have been told? Or was it a myth for us to understand? We can see that the fall of Adam is the complete foundation of this entire Christian religion; without it there would be no need for atonement nor the death of the Son. To believe in the "Fall" one must believe in the literal, six-day creation of the world, and that Adam was created wholly as the first man on the sixth day of a very busy week. This belief must ignore all scientific facts and theories of a world millions of years old, and that the word "Adam" meant mankind, plural instead of singular. It requires the belief in a God of form and similarity of traits to man to condemn and sentence him and all of his generations for another's crime.

If these things happened over a period of ages as taught by other ancient writings that are fully as believable, and by proven scientific fact, then the "Fall" was only the symbol of the evolution of mankind from an unintelligent Homo Sapiens specie to a thinking, free-willed being, though simple of mind and consciousness, awakening to the realization of being.

We realize that the True grace of God has never been understood. There are no qualifications to be met in true Grace. True grace was shown by the father of the Prodigal Son. Nor can Divine Love and wisdom be gained in any other way but by true grace. These latter are the rewards for diligent seeking after Truth. These are essences, the intrinsic nature of the universal intelligence and energy that permeates the totality of space and every form therein. These essences with others is what lifts us to God-likeness, or Christ-like.

The God and Satan of religion is a belief created in man's mind of Spirit Beings creating and ruling the world. Man could then blame Satan, the God of Evil, for his faults and weaknesses and could turn to God, through the priesthood, for forgiveness for his failure. But man CAN overcome his weaknesses through the god-power within his intuitional inner Self as we have seen in so many lives of utter despair. This is the message that must be taught; that help is always there in time of need - if we find the way to truly seek it.

But instead, we have been taught to believe that we are guilty in the eyes of God from the very moment of birth. The only guilt that we should have is for being so slow to learn the will of the Spirit within, so that we will not have to repeat our classes of living so many times.

Yes, we are wrong in our ways of life, but we have not been taught the true way. The Father, however, deep within us, is patient, "full of grace and truth". "He" waits for us to learn.

Did not the Father, in the parable of the Prodigal Son, wait patiently for the son to change his mind and his ways and RETURN? The son thought that he was separated from the Father, but the Father's love - and grace - was always with him. He was always a son. Man cannot understand this kind of Divine Love, never accusing but always waiting for the mind to be renewed.

We must look deeper into this mystery to understand the true grace of God. It is not an accuser. It is not a forgiver. Think for a moment of the story of the harlot brought before Jesus to be accused. He did not accuse her. He rebuked those who did. He did not say, "I forgive you." He knew and she knew that her ways were improper. Jesus said very gently, "Neither do I condemn thee. Go and sin no more." He was not her judge. Her accusers fled for they, too, had their own hidden problems, and she turned her life to following Jesus and His teachings.

God is not our accuser. This Great Creative Intelligence is our patient Father and Teacher deep within us. Who, then, is our accuser? Our own carnal mind - and the pious ones around us. We have been told for centuries that we are sinners from the very moment of birth, instead of being told that we are here to learn and evolve. We have believed the former tale and lived with the guilt, but there was never a hint of our real assignment

233

through the school of experience. Let us examine these facts from a new and different viewpoint.

This Grace of God gave man two gifts as his mind began to develop beyond only intuition as the animals, so that he could willfully learn the Way. These were the ability to think (reason) and the freedom of will. We read in the myths of Genesis that Eve "saw" the "fruit" of the Tree of Knowledge of Good and Evil, that it looked good (reasoning) and that she partook (freedom of will). Through inquisitiveness and weakness Adam willingly partook with her, and they both realized they were "naked", without the covering of intuition.

This has been called "the fall of Man" by western theology. Strangely enough, it is the belief only of the western, civilized world. But it reeks with symbolism. It is time now for us to cast aside these spiritual leaders of myths and use our the great reasoning power given us.

This was the evolving of the Homo species toward a godlike, conscious creature, able to discern and create. It has been a long, slow process of learning to control these gifts of freedom and desires in the manner they were designed, just as a child struggles to learn the control of its body. But the control must come over our minds and over our desires through the guidance of our patient inner Teacher as we lift our consciousness to a higher level. This is the striving to carry the yoke offered us.

We have never thought nor have we been taught of this era of infancy in the long, drawn-out evolution of mankind as a specie. This was the time as spoken of in Genesis when man was turned out of the Garden for eating an apple. Actually, man had only discovered himself as a separate entity. He was an individual, conscious of being conscious of the world of form. He could barely think, and he could barely will. This began the long arduous trek through the world of experience from the innocence of being led by his unconscious much like an animal to the wisdom of today, a trek that has taken many ages of time.

Though he no doubt felt bewildered and lost, man was never alone. There was always a myriad of angels and hierarchies surrounding him to guide him by his intuition. These were the higher waves of energy coming to him from outer space. For where else could they have come?

"And the Elohim said, "Behold, the man has become as one of us, to know good and evil . . ." By this act he lifted himself from a gardener to become, in time, as a god, knowing good and evil. He became under the Law of Cause and effect. No longer was he as the animals; his brain was developing and, through trial and error, he was beginning to use it. But this was his destiny from the beginning; to learn to manifest the ways of the Father and become a Creative Being.

Science assumes there must be other solar systems with planets also circling their suns somewhere in the vastness of our Milky Way galaxy with its billions of suns. Perhaps millions more in the billions of galaxies in the vastness of the universe. If this is so, and the probabilities are extremely high, no doubt there are millions of planets with life forms very similar to ours. Did all of them - or even some of them - "fall out of grace with "God" as we seem to have done? The odds are quite high that this might very well could have happened, if that was God's plan of creation. Did God also create a sacrificial Son for every one of those planets? Surely, we could not have been the only planet with rebellious children. Reasoning seems to ask us to re-examine our beliefs and seek a new understanding.

As we open this new century and a new millennium it is time for us to begin using the reasoning powers given to us to examine our old beliefs and understand the MEANINGS of the myths of yesteryears. It is time to make whatever changes it takes to seek the next level of truth for each of us.

"I stand at the door and knock; If any man hear my voice and open the door, I will come into him and will sup with him, and he with Me." There is no hint that the Father within would only knock once or twice and leave. All that is required is to open the door of our mind and sup with Him(seek and listen).

We now realize that the grace of God is the patient waiting for man to hear that wee small voice within, to realize his carnal, materialistic ways, to lift his mind to a higher realm of thinking and begin doing the "will of the Father" within. Time is not the essence. We are accuser and the judge of ourselves, for what we sow we also reap. Nothing more; nothing less. Thus we begin to understand the *Grace of God.*

-22-

The Divine Plan

Everyone who gazes lovingly upon a rose is not similarly affected by its radiance and beauty. Nor does a work of art bring a similar emotional feeling to all those who share it. Such beauty and grandeur is only in the eye of the beholder, for these are essences that move only our senses.

The object could even be a symbol of the dim past, and though we do not hold it in our conscious mind, it can still dwell deep within our intuition, our inner consciousness, and we still hold it dear whenever it is viewed. Such we find in ancient religious forms that we still hold in reverence. Some of these are the cross, the dove, the virgin mother holding a child, and other symbols that date back into antiquity, into the ancient days of Egypt and Persia. These can bring an inner experience even to a gathering of people gazing upon them, for they bring to mind the spiritual Self deep within that man inwardly longs for.

Through our intuition we still live in the world of myth and symbols, and they remain the only link to that other higher world, the world of Thought and Vision. The meanings are still unknown to us, but we worship the unknown as mankind has for ages of time. It is our link to the past that we have forgotten through time.

We are not seeking this inner world, however. Our carnal minds know nothing of it. We have heard the mythology and have been shown the symbols in our religious life, but in reality it is an unattainable world for the carnal mind. The nonchalant attitude we have toward the spiritual attest to this. Only a bare handful, figuratively speaking, of the millions of Christians are actually striving for the perfection it requires which is a new rebirth in our thinking, our lives and our desires.

We are instead seeking the thrill and experiences of being alive and the thrill of attainment of that which will broaden this feeling of grandeur. We turn, then, from the symbols that contain the deeper understanding of life to the easier salvation of faith that theology offers us. We turn away from our intuition in which the vision of the true Plan of Life can come, from the Father within which Jesus spoke of, and accept a plan formed by the early Council of Man.

Why is this?

There can be only one true reason. The images we have been given by our religious leaders are of a heaven above and the earth below, with the sun and the moon and a few sprinkled stars as luminaries. There is little effort involved as it only requires to be accepted by faith alone. We have not caught the vision of universal oneness, full of love and charity as the teachings of Jesus revealed to His followers.

But the fairy tales that we have been immersed in are growing passe' to a greater number of people as they search for the "meat" of spiritual teachings that shows, as Jesus said, "My yoke is easy and my burden is light." We must find the way to come into the Light of Understanding and not be led further into the Wilderness.

The gods of the past throughout the world were War Gods, teaching the Law of Survival to the people. The God of the Hebrews, Jehovah, which was accepted by Christianity as the one true God, is an example of this type as He supposedly led "His" people into their wars of conquest and slaughter of their enemies. This has been referred to as the "Law of the Fish." The big fish live off the little ones, and the little ones must be numerous and fast to survive. Thus we find the multitude of people among the weaker while the bigger ones, though a minority, live off them through business and tithing.

This is the pattern. The strong and powerful hold the weaker in bondage. Where did the teachings of religion, then, loose Love and Charity, the real inner teachings of Jesus? It was lost in the development of ritual worship by the priesthood for control of people's mind instead of the development of a way of life for the creation of a more perfect society.

Now the divine plan is again being revealed. When we realize that our thoughts and desires are in reality forming our future life, we should begin to see the light of a better way. So far, our carnal nature has led us down this rock-strewn and pot-holed road we call life, never realizing there must be some recompense for our actions. But now we are beginning to hear that there is a time of payment, an effect for every cause we bring forth. Balance must reign. It is time for us to open our eyes to the tremendous possibilities that could lie ahead - if we would change our thinking.

Understanding comes slowly. Sometimes it can be very painful as we must admit that believing something is not always the answer. I have finally realized that what I "believe" is not always the answer. It does not make anything true - or untrue. It usually reveals a closed mind. Now I surmise that many things are possible, and I must weigh everything in the light of reason and experience, and accept that which seems possible. I must walk in the light I am given, and continually search for more than just the candle I now possess.

Truth, we find, is nebulous. What is truth to us today will turn into only a step toward a deeper truth tomorrow. We need only review the advancement in knowledge during this past century to see that theories and beliefs of yesteryear was only a step toward the truth of today. It has brought us to a realization of the vastness of space that we never dreamed possible. It has brought us to an era of possibilities in the medical field that has brought relief and longevity to many. The airplane's ability to fly in the thinness of air proved far more than a dream.

We are finding that there is really no end to what the mind of man can visualize and create. There is a new vision waiting for the masses to realize the possibilities that exist - if we fasten our minds to a higher realm of thought. The heavenly throne has become trillions of miles across, filled with uncountable numbers of nuclear furnaces (suns) blazing and exploding. There are particles smaller than the protons and electrons of the atom being discovered under our powerful microscopes.

We are finding that man has become a triune self instead of only flesh and blood, to drop away in a short time. He has become a living soul, with the inner dream of a beautiful life somewhere in the future. It is not a myth; it is a vision of a possibility that we can strive for. The archetype is already in our mind. The way of attainment is now coming forth. It is the oneness of all in true charity. "That ye love one another as I have loved you."

We are beginning to grasp the concept of the Divine Plan of Creation that marked the beginning of time. We realize how things have evolved from the simplicity of pure energy to the complexity of form as motion began. We can suddenly realize and appreciate the meaning of life. It is the continual motion of the latent energy to become the model of the archetype, the body of the Christ Spirit formed in humanity. It is kinetic energy in a form to create toward perfection. Mankind as a whole, not individually as we have been trying to do, has the ultimate aim to become that body for the Christ Spirit - in time.

The more it is examined the more probable this divine plan becomes, manifesting this Universal Consciousness in form, from useless latent energy into kinetic energy of usefulness. As stated in some of the aged manuscripts of India, "Before the beginning, the Father/Mother was asleep in quiet Chaos, of nothingness". It was just latent energy. "Then the Mother brought the Son, movement". The first movement of this energy brought forth the basic elements of matter. Formation began, from the single atom of hydrogen into every metal imaginable through the extreme heat of nuclear fusion in the countless suns, into forms of usefulness for the entities of life. Thus was the beginning of evolution as we have been shown through scientific studies.

Genesis gives us no plan, only a summary. All we have is the analogy given us of a six-day creation that was given up so quickly and so easily through an act of minor disobedience. Now we have a hint of an evolving creation through many eras of time, from the chaos of latent energy to the building of matter and life forms. Dimly, we can faintly imagine a divine plan of work for formation, or a continual fusion throughout the universe if we state it more bluntly. It is a far cry from the myth of "fallen Adam". But out of this has come to us the ability to choose between "good" and "evil" under the Karmic Law of Cause and Effect. The choice is ours, as is the payment and/or the reward for our choice and action.

It decrees that we understand that the decisions we make are of our own choosing, and that we must bear the consequences. We believe now that we have a way out through confession and forgiveness. But in analysis, we must realize that our actions have already had their effect, and these cannot be reversed as if they never happened. Nor can a cause be exempt and forgiven by a sudden feeling of remorse or a death-bed repentance. We can regret, and strive for goodness to balance the seeds we plant.

Let us turn for a moment to the scene of Jesus and the harlot that was brought before him for judgment. Jesus did not accuse her of sinning, nor did he forgive her for anything. He told her politely, "go and sin no more".

There are many mysteries that have gone unanswered in our beliefs. Such a one is death and rebirth. We are beginning to realize that "we" are not the body, but rather we are the soul which is tucked "somewhere" within the body, that which gives the commands to move - or not to move. It thinks. It is the objective mind. It is a conscious spirit entity. But where does it go upon death of the body? Does it just passively join trillions of other souls that have separated from their bodies, to wait patiently for Judgment Day and the great Eternal bonfire we are told that is facing the transgressors?

Jesus explains this in John 9:1-3. His disciples asked him if the blind man on the street had sinned to have caused this blindness, or was it his parents. Jesus answered, "Neither has this man sinned, nor his parents, but that the works of God could be made manifest." It was the Law of Karma at work. In a previous life this soul must have had accumulated Karma that was still unpaid at death, so in his next incarnation he must serve it out.

At another time Jesus asked the disciples who people thought that he previously was, and they named some of the prophets. He also showed the disciples the spirits (souls) of Abraham and Moses, standing together.

The story of Job is truly one to examine in our hours of trials. In his afflictions Job cried out to God, "If a man dies, shall he live again?" He had fallen from his high, righteous life to a life of deep sorrow. In his ignorance he justified his pious life and blamed God for his circumstances.

"Then God answered Job out of the whirlwind, and said, 'Who is this that darkened council by words without knowledge? Gird up thine loins like a man; for I will demand of thee, and answer thou me. Where were you when I laid the foundations of the earth? Declare, if thou hast understanding."

It is well to read this 38th chapter through the 40th of this great book. We find the omnipotence and the marvelous unveiling of the divine plan of the power and how cause and effect has balanced evolution . Everything is ruled by immutable Law. Righteousness and balance, continually upward, has been the ruling force.

As Job reasoned with the God within him, he realized that there was much of God's plan that he didn't know, and that God was still in control of the universe. Meekly, he accepted his plight and answered, "I have heard of thee by the hearing of my ear, but now mine eyes seeth thee." His mind was opened to a new understanding. "Wherefore I abhor myself and repent in dust and ashes." He was now a man completely reborn by reasoning his condition and realizing that his "righteousness" was at fault and not the Laws of the universe.

So many of us have not realized the omnipotence of the Universal Consciousness that is continually creating away, slowly but surely toward its goal of the Christ Spirit in all things, a new world. It has not lost its first creation to a mythical Satan, or to a fallen Angel, Lucifer. The universe that began 15 billion years ago is still in the state of progression. Maybe the time will come in the far, far distant future when it will slowly come to a stop, and turn once again back into its One Point of Nothingness as before, but that, too, will be another tale to tell around some far distant campfire.

Job's first theory of righteousness brought him only a high and pious life and would not stand the test of Karma. When changes came to his life he blamed God for his misfortunes, never realizing that a cause lay somewhere in his own past.

Salvation as a theory also does not stand the test of true annalysis. It requires the story of the fall of Adam. It also requires the immaculate birth of Jesus and his sacrificial death upon the cross at Calvary for the sins of the world, acceptance of which is "salvation".

So, too, do we find that Evolution by itself does not stand alone. Nor does Karma. Nor does Rebirth. Together, however, we begin to understand the divine plan of the advancement of Consciousness from chaos to a more perfect way as a body for the Christ spirit. They do not lead to a nebulous Heaven, but they do explain why the many differences in births and life's circumstances that otherwise must be left to "Chance", the gambler's game. We can begin to realize that there was an "archetype" of Paradise created in the beginning, and Consciousness has been slowly forming the fishes, the birds, the animals, and finally man to inhabit it.

Think once more of the great worldly stage upon which we all must trod, each playing our parts to the best of our ability - and our understanding. But is this spirit given only one short curtain call before judgment of our true abilities, with the expectation of performing each scene perfectly without any true direction? I dare say that it would be a foolish test.

It is the soul of mankind that is evolving, that ray of spirit that began as latent energy to become a useful form, for here is the true "I". As the soul evolves, so also does its culture, its environment, and even the vessel which it fashions for its use. Thus we see the body of today's man/woman far more capable and refined than in past centuries because of a different need. He has built an environment for more comfort and pleasure. But, sadly, his beliefs have basically remained a constant, that of worshipping gods created in his mind, and holding his evolution at a meager rate through the lack of true guidance of the spirit, the Father within.

Many are the vessels the soul has tried down through time to no avail. All have proven faulty, corruptible, and full of ignorance. All have been discarded in death. Each, of course, strived in its allotted time to satisfy its carnal mind, to direct its will to be righteous in its own pattern, and refusing to recognize the Director within, waiting to teach it its true part to play. So it has continued, from birth to death and to birth again, returning to the schoolhouse of life, but still following the same pattern of the carnal mind directing the will.

Such is the Grace and the patience of the Director, patiently waiting for us to see the light and seek the true way.

This is certainly not an attempt to bring forth a new doctrine; the world is filled with such. But there are new thoughts and new understanding of the writings of the ancient mystics that are coming forth at this time. They convey the meaning to many of the beliefs that have been formed down through time. It reveals a new vision for mankind of the possibility of a new world and the Brotherhood of mankind. But first it takes the vision of the possibilities before the little bird can fly, or the child to walk, or before mankind can create all that which he can see in his mind.

Perhaps the day will come when we can say, as Job so meekly said, "I have heard of thee by the hearing of my ear, but now mine eyes (the inner vision) seeth thee. I abhor myself (for my piety) and repent in dust and ashes." (Parentheses added.)

Perhaps should be added our own words from our hearts, "I accept the destiny that I have built."

Now, as I dwell upon these thoughts, the words of my dear Mother come to me through these many years. It is not the Sunday School lesson of Adam and Eve, not the story of Moses leading his flock through the desert. It is the continual admonition that she strove to instill into her offspring as perhaps her Mother instilled into her.

"Watch that tongue of yours!" "Behave yourself!" "Don't tease your baby sister. Love her!" And most important of all was her teaching, "We are all children of God. We should love one another!"

How I have thanked her for the guidance she so lovingly gave!

EPILOGUE

Some might feel that I have been far too critical of the early Roman Church and of the Christianity that came out of it. What I have written is only the recorded history that can be found in the reference books in one's own library. It is not as criticism; it is striving to reveal the manner in which our beliefs have been formed, a step that must be taken for the revelation to come to many.

I would rather have it spoken of if at all as a memorial to all the millions of souls that were tortured and murdered in heinous ways for only believing differently. This slaughter of innocent people down through the centuries was carried on by the very "Christian" organization that claimed to be God's infallible messenger to the people. We find it to have been only a governmental appointed organization of power-hungry individuals who enslaved the people through their religious teachings.

Only a few of man's religions have taught above all things the absolute demand of a life of love for all in order to be called Godly. Sadly, Christianity is not one of them. It is a theology based upon faith in its concept of a fall from grace by Adam and the salvation offered by their

247

belief in the sacrifice of God's only begotten son, certainly not taught by Jesus.

Two examples of these barbarous acts are the burning at the stake of both Joan of Arc and Giordano Bruno, the Itallian poet of the 16th century, only two of millions. The former was executed by burning because she felt that God led her more than church doctrine. She was branded heretical for this and also for continuing to dress in male clothing, strictly forbidden by the church. Later she was tried in absentia (after she was burned to death) and was found innocent. Later, she was connonized and sainted. We see here an effect that could not be reverse (her death), although the cause was forgiven by the pope.

Giodano Bruno (1548 - 1600) became dissatisfied with the dogma of the church and began studying Plato, Pythagoras, and Hermes. His studies led him to the theory of the circulation of the blood that was later proved to be correct. He later taught Philosophy at the University of Paris and lectured in London on the Copernicus theory of helie-centric as being a new theory of scientific thought. For this teaching he was accused of heresy by an Inquisition court, tortured and imprisoned for over 7 years. Finally he was taken out of proson and executed by burning.

Ironically, there stands close to the Vatican in Rome a statue in his memory, in the very spot where he was executed by the church, erected 2 centuries later by the liberation movement.

These atrocities were done under the banner of Christianity according to the Roman Catholic Church, that organization that claims to be the mediator betweeen God and man, and who declares itself infallible. But now these atrocities and the theology it professes are being revealed by history and acience.

Knowing these facts and its clinging to the the myths of Adam's fall and the 7-day creation 6000 years ago leaves me no alternative but to turn from it and the Christianity it began centuries ago.

I find that the progression of Consciousness through matter, from the initial protons and neutrons of the scientific theory of the Beginning to the present Homo Sapiens a far more reasonable theory to live by. It needs no blood sacrifices for salvation, and it has hope for all. The teachings of Jesus, of loving one another and the kindom of God within each of us as a guide to a more perfect way, seems a more perfect way.

One thing that we can be sure of is that change is a continuing process and knowledge is spreading. Old ideas are fast fading away and the vision of a new world is filling the hearts of more and more people over the horizon.

It is my sincere hope to glimpse the day when we shall all turn to loving one another for what we are, God's children, and not continue in the horrible caste system that we have formed down through time. For only then will we truly be "born again", from the world of Individualism which we are immersed into a world of Oneness, the Kingdom of God. For only then will suffering cease and tears of joy fill the eyes of the oppressed, and "the lion will lie down with the lamb."

About the Author

Author Raymond Moyer's interest in religion began at the very early age of four months, as attested by the Cradle Call certificate that still hangs on his wall. It was awarded to him by the Methodist Church in the small cattle town of Roundup, Montana where he was born. It was also at this early age that his father was killed in an oil field accident, and soon after began the family's trek to western Washington.

He served in World War 2 as a bombardier over Europe, but instead of dropping bombs he dropped propaganda and surrender leaflets on the enemy. Married, raised four children, and finally, in 1964, settled in Vancouver, Washington. After 20 years in the accounting world, he retired into the service station business for 6 years, and 4 years as a real estate agent. Finally, in 1982 he and his wife completely retired and spent 8 months driving throughout the entire United States.

Printed in the United States
41560LVS00003B/522